WATER DEVELOPMENT, SUPPLY AND MANAGEMENT

Series Editor: ASIT K. BISWAS

Volume 7

WATER AND SOCIETY

CONFLICTS IN DEVELOPMENT

Part 1

The Social and Ecological Effects of Water Development
in Developing Countries

WATER DEVELOPMENT, SUPPLY AND MANAGEMENT

Other titles in the series:

NOTICE TO READERS

Dear Reader

If your library is not already a standing order customer or subscriber to this series, may we recommend that you place a standing or subscription order to receive immediately upon publication all new issues and volumes published in this valuable series. Should you find that these volumes no longer serve your needs your order can be cancelled at any time without notice.

The Editors and the Publisher will be glad to receive suggestions or outlines of suitable titles, reviews or symposia for consideration for rapid publication in this series.

ROBERT MAXWELL
Publisher at Pergamon Press

WATER AND SOCIETY

CONFLICTS IN DEVELOPMENT

Part 1

The Social and Ecological Effects of Water Development
in Developing Countries

Editor

CARL WIDSTRAND

*Scandinavian Institute of African Studies
Uppsala, Sweden*

PERGAMON PRESS
OXFORD · NEW YORK · TORONTO · SYDNEY · PARIS · FRANKFURT

U.K.	Pergamon Press Ltd., Headington Hill Hall, Oxford OX3 0BW, England
U.S.A.	Pergamon Press Inc., Maxwell House, Fairview Park, Elmsford, New York 10523, U.S.A.
CANADA	Pergamon of Canada Ltd., 75 The East Mall, Toronto, Ontario, Canada
AUSTRALIA	Pergamon Press (Aust.) Pty. Ltd., 19a Boundary Street, Rushcutters Bay, N.S.W. 2011, Australia
FRANCE	Pergamon Press SARL, 24 rue des Ecoles, 75240 Paris, Cedex 05, France
FEDERAL REPUBLIC OF GERMANY	Pergamon Press GmbH, 6242 Kronberg-Taunus, Pferdstrasse 1, Federal Republic of Germany

First edition 1978

HD
1702
W35
1978

British Library Cataloguing in Publication Data

Water and society, conflict in development.
Part 1: The social and ecological effects of
water development in developing countries.
(Water development, supply and management; Vol. 7).
1. Underdeveloped areas - Water resources
development - Social aspects - Congresses
I. Widstrand, Carl II. Series
333.9'1'0091724   HD1702   78-40346
ISBN 0-08-022447-4

First published in the journal *Water Supply and Management,* Volume 2 Number 4,
1978 and supplied to subscribers as part of their subscription.

Printed in Great Britain by A. Wheaton & Co Ltd, Exeter, Devon

TABLE OF CONTENTS

PREFACE

The studies in the present volume were presented at a seminar on the social aspects of water exploitation in developing countries organized within the framework of a research project "Water Related Problems in Developing Countries". This project aims at providing a survey of knowledge of the exploitation of water resources in Africa and the Indian sub-continent. The project is financed by the Swedish Agency for Research Cooperation with Developing Countries (SAREC) and the Swedish Committee for Future-Oriented Research (SALFO). The survey will be concentrated on two major areas of concern: problems of arranging water supply for urban and rural populations and problems of irrigated agriculture.

Quite early in the work on this survey it became clear that the social effects of water development and the range of social processes which influence the planning and exploitation of water resources have received little attention in the literature compared to the mass of existing research on the technological and physical performance of water projects. We have therefore focused our attention on social aspects and the survey of knowledge is conceived as a study on conflicts in the use and development of water resources. It will be published as a companion volume.

Our interest in the social aspects of water exploitation also led to the organizing of the seminar to which we invited research workers with a long-standing interest in this topic. The seminar was held at the University of Uppsala and the Scandinavian Institute of African Studies at Uppsala, Sweden, 24-26 October, 1977.

The invited scientists presented their papers to a public meeting of some 150 persons interested in water research, water consultancies, water management, and development cooperation and research. Two days were spent in discussions with a small group. Some of the points raised in the papers and some of the research ideas brought forward are presented in an introduction to the studies. Essential ideas expressed during the seminar discussions will be taken up in the companion volume.

It is our pleasant duty to convey our thanks to the University of Uppsala and to the Secretary of the Project Committee, Lennart de Maré and the staff of the Scandinavian Institute of African Studies, who technically organized the seminar.

Malin Falkenmark
Executive Secretary
of the Committee of
Hydrology,
Natural Science
Research Council.

Gunnar Lindh
Professor, Head of
the Dept of
Water Resources
Engineering,
University of Lund.

Carl Gösta Widstrand
Director,
Scandinavian
Institute of
African Studies.

Water Supply & Management, Vol. 2, pp. 279-282.
© Pergamon Press Ltd., 1978. Printed in Great Britain.

0364-7714/78/0801-0279$02.00/0

Social and Economic Aspects of Water Exploitation

C. WIDSTRAND

This issue discusses economic and social aspects in the widest sense of irrigation programmes and projects aimed at providing drinking water for rural people. It is basically focused on the Indian subcontinent and Eastern Africa.

Over the last century vast amounts of resources have gone into the construction of large-scale irrigation works on the Indian subcontinent. Over the last 10 years several donor countries have contributed substantial amounts of funds and technical expertise for the provision of urban and rural water installations in Eastern Africa. Yet, during recent years it has been shown quite clearly that the expected social benefits from drinking water supplies have not been realized and that irrigation projects have created more problems than they solve. None have fulfilled the expectations of planners and governments and most projects are used only to 50% of their capacity. This means that 100 million ha of land with available irrigation are not used and that millions of rural people who are provided with pumps, pipes and installations cannot get any water out of them. This issue is concerned with why this has happened and what can be done about it.

The provision of *drinking water* to rural East Africa has long been a preoccupation of Scandinavian donor agencies. Originally the idea was that development depended on a satisfactory health situation and the health situation depended in turn on the supply of clean water. Women spent too much time on drawing and carrying water, and their burden should be made easier. Health improvement has not been that dramatic, as Richard Feachem's article shows. The reason for this is quite simple: if you are not aware of the necessity to separate feces and water, or rather if you fail to do so, there are so many other ways of polluting your drinking water before you drink it that it is useless to supply clean water to start with. Women have to go more often to the new well or the tap as it is closer and tend to spend the same amount of time drawing water as before, now without the help of children and youngsters.

We do not really know if people take their water from the new source during the whole year or only during the dry season. There may be water sources closer at hand during the wet season. We have no idea what children drink and children under 5 years of age have the highest death rate due to diarrheal diseases. Some of us have heard people say that this spring water, which is so cold that it hurts your teeth, might be alright for cattle and goats but that water for humans should be brown and murky, it should smell and be more filling because that is the way it has been for generations.

And finally, the pumps do not work regularly or the pressure in the communal taps varies or peters out. People tend to avoid unreliable sources of water. In any case they will try to avoid paying for their use, and rightly so. (After all, God provides the water and we did the digging, so why shouldn't the government provide the pipes free?)

There are several reasons for this situation. One is that the provision of water supplies has been almost exclusively in the domain of engineers, with a light sprinkling of economists. This in turn meant an initial emphasis on the production of technical installations from boreholes to sophisticated purification plants. Size and quantity was important, there were so many people to provide water for. Questions about operation and maintenance were put off until the future. Furthermore, the provision of water was seen as a donor-to-government operation rather than donor-to-people. This in turn meant that the planning and siting of supplies was planned from above and the local people had no say whatsoever. This of course makes things easier for the donors who can bundle the provision of engineers, pipes, pumps, drilling rigs, taps and nuts into a neat package with a fixed price. The propensity for quick technological fixes was very obvious in the early and middle sixties, and little thought went into finding out what people wanted to have, or into rudimentary education programmes on water use, hygiene or into simple training programmes for pump attendants or water installation repairmen.

Now, 10-15 years later, we are suffering from this lack of minimal vision about the future. *Operation and maintenance* (which are not the same thing!) should ideally have been a local responsibility. But this costs money which wasn't there, nor was it forthcoming from donors, where interest in this respect has been negligible, except for the Swedish International Development Authority (SIDA), which has provided funds for maintenance over recent years. So, maintenance has been the responsibility of a small group of over-worked and underfunded local engineers and a motley of dedicated volunteers.

Local planning is very important if the local inhabitants are to feel a responsibility for some common useful resource, such as pumps or water installations. If there is no feeling that this is "ours" and that it is important that it works for the common good, there will be no-one to take responsibility for the installation, for looking after delivery of diesel fuel for the pump or for calling a repairman.

The lessons for the planners and donors are obvious: more funds and more resources into public health training and education (with local teachers), more funds into training programmes for operators and maintenance personnel—not producing full-scale engineers, but, instead, small-scale mechanics with some basic skills directly applicable to the water system—and more thought about the involvement of locals in the planning of water schemes. There are, of course, many other questions which have only been partly touched upon in this volume: pricing of water and the regulation of water consumption through pricing, legal institutions, differential pricing, other back-up activities in the education field, problems of political will, trade-offs between water programmes and other important programmes etc.

More *water for irrigation* and more land under irrigation is a necessity if we are to be able to feed enormously increasing populations. We can then immediately identify many problems, of which two are discussed at length in this issue by Obeng, Bottrall and Carruthers. The first is the problem of disease which follows irrigation and installations like dams which sometimes are necessary to provide height for gravity schemes. Malaria and schistosomiasis are some of the worst debilitating diseases of man, which immediately follow irrigation projects. A major effort is now being made through the WHO to channel funds to basic and applied research concerning these and related diseases. Again, no research on schistosomiases will help unless people are made aware that it is spread via urine or feces. But the education problem is formidable.

The other problem is, in a way, a contradiction built into the water administration system. On the one hand, administration has to regulate the water flow according to the availability of water, on the other hand, it has to allocate water according to the real needs of the different units. In schemes where you deal with farmers who own their land (India, Pakistan) there is no easy way of controlling what crops they choose to grow, whereas this may be easier in African schemes where tenants are much more dependent on the management of the scheme, and where the scheme decides crops and crop rotation.

Technological development has also made the position of the administration stronger, although the management systems as they are today cannot really meet the demands of modern agriculture and modern crops that need precise amounts with precise timing. As Robert Chambers has said, the green revolution did not turn red, it turned brown.

If the administration cannot satisfactorily meet the two contradictory allocation problems mentioned above, water will become an important factor when it comes to the distribution of economic and political power. The wealth-concentrating effects of water are very real.

We have very little information on some of the aspects of irrigation management, especially on those who manage those who manage water, i.e. the middle echelons in the water hierarchies. As Bottrall points out, there are remarkably large returns to be had from slight improvements in management systems, but this has been a sadly neglected field. A problem related to it is mentioned by Carruthers who says that the study of institutions benefiting from irrigation (such as norms, rules of conduct and generally accepted ways of doing things) is another neglected field. He emphasizes that the planning and indeed, the transfer of irrigation technology must include not only the hardware but also the software of institutions, services and attitudes.

I have said earlier that developments in the water field have been dominated by engineers with some scientists and economists added: people who can provide figures and hard facts. The problems outlined above (and indeed in this issue) are software problems, the prerogative of sociologists and anthropologists. So, the easy answer to some of the questions seems to be: why were social scientists not consulted before household water projects were started, why are they not used in irrigation studies etc? Yes, why?

There are several reasons for this. One is a vital lack in the training programme of social scientists. They are taught to observe and comment or shoot or snipe from the sideline, but they are never taught any normative decision-making. Again, it is a matter of your personal politics whether you think this or that is good or bad. The easy way out is to observe and comment, *post festum*. This is why it is so difficult to bring in social scientists at the beginning of a project because they will have difficulties knowing what their input should be. In most cases such people are also hired from universities to do short term consultancies and they do not know the restrictions in time, policy, and other aspects of the agency they are hired by. As the methods are more time consuming than the simple use of calculators, engineers most often begin by demanding too much from them and end up by not demanding anything at all. In my opinion agencies would do better if they had a "resident" social scientist for mutual adult education. Social scientists in most cases certainly need to explain what they are doing, what their methods are and indeed, they have to learn quite a lot of the technical and scientific aspects of water projects. Unless they have an understanding of technical processes they are likely to come up with findings which, according to Bottrall, are exciting to them but will tend to be banal and predictable to most people with extensive practical experience of irrigation management. It takes a special kind of person, for whom training is not yet provided, to take part in interdisciplinary teams. This is a comment which returns at regular intervals in this issue.

There is a vast array of social theory and, in my opinion, one of the urgent problems confronting social scientists today is to chart the way by which this lode of theory can be mined for explanations and generalizations. Whether this would be labelled as applied research or something else does not bother me unduly, it is badly needed at the present time if we are to come from understanding to prescription and from prescription to action in many of the social aspects of water exploitation.

Water Supply & Management, Vol. 2, pp. 283-297.
© Pergamon Press Ltd., 1978. Printed in Great Britain.

0364-7714/78/0801-0283$02.00/0

Environmental Implications of Water Development for Developing Countries

ASIT K. BISWAS

Water, said the Greek philosopher Pindar, as early as the fifth century BC, is the best of all things. It may perhaps be an overstatement, but it is certainly not surprising since it has always been regarded as one of the most precious commodities throughout man's recorded history. Water makes human, animal and plant life possible, and without it, life and civilization, at least the way it is known today, cannot develop or survive.

Another Greek philosopher, Empedocles of Agrigentum (490-430 BC), postulated that water was one of the four primary elements or roots, *rhizomata*, from which all materials of the world were constituted. The other three basic elements were air, fire and earth. The last two elements, in the present circumstances, may be regarded as equivalent to energy and land or soil. Thus, in a very real sense the early Greek philosophers hit upon the four basic elements that enter into all fundamental considerations associated with the human environment. Thus, water was accepted as an important element and was further considered to be one of the fundamental building blocks of nature. Even great philosophers like Plato and Aristotle accepted this concept of water as a fundamental element with only minor modifications (Biswas, 1972).

It is possible to write the entire history of mankind in terms of man's need for water. From the very beginning, it was realized that water was an essential ingredient for survival, and hence, early civilizations developed and flourished on lands made fertile by major rivers—the Tigris and the Euphrates in Mesopotamia, the Nile in Egypt, the Indus in the Indian subcontinent and the Huang-Ho in China.

WATER AND THE ENVIRONMENT

From early days, man soon realized that rivers and streams, in their natural states, seldom provided adequate water to satisfy his needs. There was either too much or too little water, resulting in floods or droughts, and both were responsible for untold misery. Consequently, water systems had to be developed by constructing dams and levees, making channel improvements or by digging canals for irrigation and drainage. The overall result was that water availability was more compatible to the human needs.

With the gradual increase in the world population, there was a corresponding need to provide more food, fibre, energy and raw materials. Also, as cities and industry developed, much of their waste was discharged to the water courses with little or no treatment, which reduced the quality of receiving waters. A direct result of such developments was a demand for more water for domestic, agricultural and industrial purposes, and at the same time the quality of much available water near centres of population deteriorated due to pollution. Hence, development and rational management of water became a prime necessity.

All development projects have environmental and economic consequences, and water development is no exception. Whether such consequences are acceptable or not are often matters of great controversy, and depend very much on the individual concerned, their personal interests, views and biases. Hence, it is not exactly uncommon to find a situation where a new water development project is unacceptable to a certain segment of the society due to unwarranted social and economic side-effects, while another segment may be lobbying hard for the same development for different reasons. To a large extent, such conflicts can be explained by an analysis of the nature of beneficiaries, which is seldom conducted for most projects. It is inevitable that any development project will benefit some citizens

Table 1. Environmental implications of water development

PHYSICAL SUB-SYSTEM

Hydrologic System	*Atmospheric System*
Water Quantity	Evaporation
	Micro-climate
Level	
Discharge	
Velocity	
Groundwater	*Crustal System*
Losses	
	Geology (soil, mineral
Water Quality	content, structure)
	Earthquake
Sediments	
Nutrients	
Turbidity	
Salinity and alkalinity	
Temperature stratification	

BIOLOGICAL SUB-SYSTEM

Aquatic Ecosystem	*Terrestrial Ecosystem*
Benthos	Submerged land and vegetation
Aufwuchs	Drawdown zone
Zooplankton	Zone above high water level
Phytoplankton	Failure impacts
Fish and aquatic vertebrates	Loss of animal habitat
Plants	Food chain repercussions
Disease vectors	

HUMAN SUB-SYSTEM

Production System	*Sociocultural System*
Agriculture	Social Costs
Fishing and hunting	Political implications
Wildlife	Anthropological effects
Recreation	
Energy	
Transportation	
Manufacturing	

more than others, and frequently some citizens may have to bear additional costs, both tangible (i.e. heavier tax liabilities) and intangible (i.e. social and environmental costs). Resolution of such conflicts, arising within the framework of democratic pluralistic societies, through political processes, is, however, the norm rather than exception.

The social and environmental consequences of water development are many, and the resulting effects often extend much further than the planning area itself. The interaction of diverse forces are often so complex that ecologists and environmentalists are hard-pressed to predict overall effects with any degree of certainty. For example, the present knowledge of ecosystems of man-made lakes leaves much to be desired. Thus, unless planning precedes construction by 5-10 years, several unpredictable and unforeseen situations tend to develop, some beneficial and others adverse. At the current state-of-the-art, environmentalists often find it impossible to convince engineers, economists and politicians that certain developments are unwise, or of the necessity to spend scarce resources on appropriate remedial measures because of lack of hard facts or solid scientific evidence. In addition, water development projects have been traditionally within the domain of engineers, and consequently social and environmental considerations have often been sadly neglected during the planning process. In certain cases, social and environmental scientists have been brought in only after the damage has become apparent (Biswas and Durie, 1971). As a rule, it is more expensive to rectify damages once they have occurred: it is cheaper to take anticipatory remedial measures. Hence, even though much lip-service is given to interdisciplinary teamwork, it is not that prevalent on a global basis.

Since the social and environmental effects of water development are many, it can be best discussed by dividing the effects on three categories of sub-systems: physical, biological and human. Table 1 provides a summary of the environmental implications of water resources development (Biswas, 1977).

PHYSICAL SUB-SYSTEM

Water development projects invariably change river and ecosystem regimes, and thus the real question is not whether such developments will affect the environment, but how much change is acceptable to society as a whole, and what countermeasures should be taken to keep the adverse changes to a minimum, at a reasonable economic cost, with that acceptable range. The Aswan Dam in Egypt, one of the largest dams of the world that was completed in 1968, has received its share of criticisms for contributing to environmental disruptions. The scheme, built primarily for generating hydropower, has produced many environmental problems. A detailed analysis of the benefits and the costs of the Aswan Dam has yet to be made, but many of these effects can now be perceived and are summarized below.

First is the question of silt. Before the dam was constructed, large amounts of silt were either deposited on the Nile Valley or carried all the way to the delta and the sea. These sediments are now being trapped in the reservoir created by the dam. Before the dam was built, suspended matter in the River Nile, passing the Aswan, ranged between 100-150 million tons per yr. Observations made during the first few years after the completion of the dam indicate that the reservoir is losing about 60 million m³ of storage per yr due to siltation. At this rate, the dead storage capacity of 30 km³ will be filled in about 500 yr.

As a result of this siltation in the reservoir, clean water is now flowing downstream to the dam causing erosion to the river bed and banks. One possibility now being considered is to construct a number of barrages to reduce the velocity and force of the clear water. These barrages can also be utilized for power generation. The other possibility is to spill the water into Toshka Depression located to the west of the lake (Hafez and Shenouda, 1978).

Another effect of the siltation in the reservoir is the erosion of the Nile Delta, some 1000 km away. Prior to the construction of the dam, the Delta used to be built up during the flood season, with the silt carried by the River to the Mediterranean. This siltation in the Delta compensated for the erosion that resulted from the winter waves of the preceding year. Without enough siltation, erosion of the Delta has become a major problem, and studies are now being carried out to find a suitable solution.

Loss of silt has further affected the productive capacity of the Nile Valley which used to get regular deposit of sediments every year. Currently studies are being undertaken to assess the actual nutritive value of the silt, and the trace elements present therein, so that this loss can be compensated by using chemical fertilizers.

Lack of sediments downstream to the dam has contributed to the significant reduction in plankton and organic carbons. It has, in turn, reduced the sardine, scombroid and crustacean population of the area. Loss of sardine along the Eastern Mediterranean has created economic problems for the fishermen who used to depend on the catch for their livelihood. Furthermore, there was a thriving small-scale industry making bricks from the silt dredged from the canals. In the absence of such silts, many such industries have now resorted to using the topsoil near the canals to make bricks, thus contributing further to the loss of productive soil in the country. Egyptian researchers have now succeeded in making bricks out of sand, but it will be some time before the local industry can be persuaded to change from using topsoil to sand. On the positive side, however, lack of silt has reduced the cost of dredging canals.

Besides siltation, other environmental problems created by the Aswan Dam that could be included within the physical sub-system, are change of terrestrial system to aquatic system, hydrometeorological effects, and changes in soil and water quality. The High Dam created a vast reservoir, having a shore-line length of 9250 km, surface area of 6216 km² and volume of 156.9 km³ at 180 m elevation. It changed 500 km of the River Nile from a riverine to lacustrine system. Though much of the land inundated was thinly populated, it contained areas rich in historical monuments, foremost of which was the Abu Simbel temple. Thus, the temples of Abu Simbel and Philae (near Aswan) had to be dismantled and moved to higher locations. The huge man-made reservoir also changed the micro-climate of the area. It was calculated that the raising of the water level by 20 m, from 160 m to 180 m, more than doubled the lake surface from 2950 km² to 6118 km², which increased the total annual evaporation from 6 km³ to 10 km³.

The construction of the High Dam and Canal system for irrigation has tended to increase the water table in many parts of Egypt. Such developments and the tendency to over-irrigate is contributing to an increase in the soil salinity problem, requiring expensive and extensive construction of drainage systems. With the disappearance of the annual Nile floods, the groundwater level has stabilized at a higher level. The salinity in the irrigation canals is increasing and some of the reclaimed lands are already facing a salination problem.

With regard to water quality of the lake, thermal stratification occurs in the summer. This, however, is to be expected since the maximum and mean depths at 180 m elevation are 130.0 m and 25.5 m, respectively. It means that the stagnant water layer at the bottom of the lake is losing dissolved oxygen which cannot be replenished, due to decomposition of organic matter. Consequently, the anaerobic biological population is taking over, which reduces nitrates to nitrites and ammonia. This is followed by sulfate reduction. Such anaerobic activity is contributing to the formation of gases like methane and hydrogen sulfide, which may interfere with water use.

The discussion of the above environmental effects of the Aswan High Dam is not meant to be a total condemnation of the structure, nor does it imply that it should never have been built. The benefits of the dam are many, and as in any other project, the benefits and costs should be compared. Increase in population and loss of productive soil has steadily decreased *per capita* cultivated land in Egypt from 0.41 acres in 1930 to 0.18 acres in 1975 (Abl Atta, 1977). The population of Egypt has increased from 20 million in 1952 to 38 million in 1976 and is expected to reach 100 million by the year 2000. Without the Aswan Dam, the situation would have been far worse. In addition, it has provided protection of the country from floods, doubled the electric power generating capacity of the country, improved river navigation, created a vast potential for fishery in Lake Nasser, more than compensating the losses of sardine along the Mediterranean coast, and enhanced the potential for tourism in the Aswan area. Thus, the real question is not whether the Aswan Dam should have been built, but rather what steps should have been taken to reduce the deleterious environmental impacts to a minimum.

There are cases where water development projects to increase irrigated agriculture have also contributed to problems which eventually reduced total food production. Among such problems are deterioration of soil fertility and eventual loss of good arable land, due to progressive development of salinity or alkalinity. For example, at one time, Pakistan alone was losing 24,280 ha of fertile cropland every year, and currently, nearly 10% of the total Peruvian agricultural area is affected by land degradation due to salination. Among other major areas affected by salination are the Helmud Valley in Afghanistan, the Punjab and Indus Valleys in the Indian sub-continent, Mexcali Valley in Northern Mexico, Imperial Valley in California and the Euphrates and Tigris basins in Syria and Iraq. A study of major modern irrigation schemes in the Punjab shows that seepage from unlined canals has, in the first 10 yr of operation, raised the water table 7-9 m above the long-term levels recorded since 1835 (Biswas and Biswas, 1977).

Water is also responsible for soil erosion, and thus it is no surprise to find that the dominant forms of soil erosion in countries like the United States are due to run-off which carries away fine sediments. Nearly 4 billion tons of sediments are carried away every year to the streams in the 48 contiguous states, nearly 75 % of which come from agricultural lands (Biswas, 1977). One-quarter of the water-borne sediments eventually end up in the oceans, but the rest remain in lakes, reservoirs and rivers, creating environmental problems. The economic cost of siltation to the United States is quite significant. Currently some 450 million yd³ of sediment are dredged every year from water bodies at a cost of about $250 million. Sediments also continually reduce the economic lives of man-made lakes which costs the nation a further $50 million annually. These, plus other damages, are estimated at approximately $500 million per yr. The total cost of soil erosion due to water is obviously much higher since the damages estimated do not include the cost of agricultural products that might have been raised, had the soil degradation not taken place. Such damages run to about 2% of the total economic value of agricultural products raised every year.

Studies carried out in Kenya during the period 1948-1965, show great variations in erosion and sedimentation in different parts of the country. Highest rates of soil erosion occurred in an area of very steep slopes on the eastern side of Mount Kenya, where land is cultivated on the steep valley slopes of the upper part of the basin, and cultivation and grazing being the dominant form of land use along the gentler but drier hill slopes of the lower parts. Thus, the annual rate of soil loss in the catchment area of the Tana River varied from 1550 tonnes/km² between Kindaruma and Grandfalls (agriculture/grazing) to about 320 tonnes/km² above Kamburu Dam (agriculture/forestry) (Ongweny, 1977). In contrast, soil erosion in undisturbed forest, in areas of steep slopes, is extremely low. For example, in the Sagana Drainage Basin, the annual rate of soil loss is approximately 4 tonnes/km². Soil loss tends to increase under agricultural conditions and is much greater in pastoral semi-arid parts of the country.

On a global scale, approximately 20 million km² of soil has been destroyed or degraded, which is nearly 35% more than the 14-15 million km² of arable land currently being used for agriculture. Currently 46% of the total degradation of the earth's surface due to different hazards can be directly related to water. These hazards can be roughly estimated as follows: water erosion, 22%; waterlogging and flood damage, 8%; salinity and alkalinity, 5%; and frost, 11%.

Finally, the possibility of inducing earthquakes by construction of large dams is another environmental problem that has not received adequate attention so far. The 1967 Koyna Dam disaster in the Indian peninsula, which resulted in a heavy loss of lives and considerable property damage, was due to an earthquake whose epicentre coincided with the dam itself. Several recent studies indicated that the observed seismic activity can be attributed directly to the creation of dams and storage reservoirs. Some of the tremors thus caused can reach magnitudes of up to six in the Richter scale and thus contribute to considerable damage. In general, the seismic disturbances can be traced to the existence of inactive faults and it seems likely that the effect of the added forces contributed by the dam and reservoir liberate orogenic tensions of much greater strength. Studies at the Kariba Dam sites appear to confirm this theory. It also appears that the height of the water column is a more important parameter in inducing earthquakes than the total volume of the reservoir. The seismic activity tends to become more pronounced once the depth exceeds 100 m (Rothe, 1973).

BIOLOGICAL SUB-SYSTEM

Water resources development can affect the biological sub-system in many different ways, and the effects can be either beneficial or adverse. Since the quality of water is of prime importance to human health, the availability of potable water to much of mankind is literally a matter of life and death. The World Health Organization (WHO) carried out a survey in 1976 on the availability of potable water in developing countries to the end of 1975. Based on the survey questionnaire that was returned by 67 developing countries, the following seems to be the current situation. In urban communities, 57% of the population have house connections and another 18% have access to standpipes, making a total of 75% (390 million people) that have access to potable water. The situation, as might be expected) is far worse for the rural sector, where only 20% (248 million) have reasonable access to safe water. If both rural and urban populations are considered, only 35% (638 million) are adequately served.

These, of course, are average figures, and hide the tremendous disparity that exists even within the developing countries. The range of this disparity can be easily seen by considering the community water supply situation in the African continent. At the upper range are several countries where more than 90% of the urban population are served by potable water. These are Botswana, Lesotho, Liberia (all 100%); Mauritius, Senegal (98%); Gambia, Guinea, Ivory Coast, Kenya, Togo, Zambia (97%); Benin, Egypt (94%); Morocco and Tunisia (91%). At the bottom end of the scale are the rural populations of several countries, where even 5% do not have access to safe water. These are Burundi, Gabon, Madagascar, Sierra Leone (1% or less); Kenya (2%); Gambia (3%); Togo and Zaire (5%). In addition, there are several other countries where data on rural sectors are not available, but they are virtually certain to be less than 5%. These are Central African Republic, Ethiopia, Guinea and Lesotho (UN Economic and Social Council, 1976).

Universal availability of potable water will undoubtedly reduce health hazards like cholera, typhoid, infectious hepatitis, amoebiasis, enterovirus diarrheas and bacillary dysentery. It would further reduce human contacts with vectors of water-borne or water-based diseases like schistosomiasis, trypanosomiasis or guinea worm (*Dracunculus medinensis*). Schistosomiasis will be discussed later. With regard to trypanosomiasis, some have estimated that the Gambian sleeping sickness, *Trypanosoma gambiense*, can be reduced by 80% by good water supply schemes (Bradley, 1974). While this figure may be somewhat optimistic, there is no doubt that the provision of potable water will reduce the incidence of the dreaded sleeping sickness disease by reducing the exposure of human beings to Tsetse flies during the water collection journey. Similarly, guinea worm infection, which currently affects some 48 million people, chiefly in India and West Africa (Müller, 1971) can also be reduced. Maximum infection occurs during dry periods, when people rely on ponds and other shallow sources. Infection rates of over 50% have been observed in India and Nigeria, and incidences of around 20-30% are commonly reported (Feachem, 1975). The health and economic costs to the communities can be substantially reduced by rational water resources development and management. It would further reduce or eliminate the time necessary for the water collection journey, which will be discussed later in the section on human sub-systems.

Water resources developments, however, do not only bring unmitigated benefits: they also often are responsible for unanticipated social costs. Thus, one of the most serious impacts of irrigation developments in the tropical and semi-tropical regions is the secondary effect of spreading water-borne diseases, and the consequent suffering of millions of human beings and animals. Irrigation schemes have often enhanced or created favourable ecological environments for parasitic and water-borne diseases such as schistosomiasis, dengue plus dengue hemorrhagic fever, liver fluke infections, Bancroftian filariasis and

Table 2. Water-borne diseases, selected examples

Parasites	Diseases transmitted	Intermediate host	Infection route
Nematoda:			
Onchocerca volvulus	River blindness (onchocerciasis)	Black fly (*Simulium* sp.)	Bite
Wuchereira bancrofti	Elephantiasis (filariasis)	Several mosquitoes	Bite
Protozoa:			
Plasmodium spp.	Malaria	Anopheles mosquito	Bite
Trypanosoma gambiense	African sleeping sickness	Tsetse fly (*Glossina* sp.)	Bite
Trematoda:			
Schistosoma haematobium	Urinary schistosomiasis (bilharziasis)	Aquatic snail (*Bulinus* sp.)	Percutaneous
Schistosoma mansoni	Intestinal schistosomiasis	Aquatic snails (*Biomphalaria*; *Australorbis*)	Percutaneous
Schistosoma japonicum	Visceral schistosomiasis	Amphibious snail (*Oncomelania*)	Percutaneous
Viruses:			
Over 30 mosquito-borne viruses are associated with human infections	Encephalitis; dengue	Several mosquitoes	Bite

malaria to flourish. These diseases are not new: for example, schistosomiasis was known during the Pharaonic times. But unprecedented expansion of perennial irrigation systems has introduced such diseases into previously uncontaminated areas. Table 2 shows some of the water-borne diseases that affect man.

Schistosomiasis is currently endemic in over 70 countries, and affects over 200 million people. Prior to the development of the present extensive irrigation networks, and when agriculture depended primarily on seasonal rainfall, the relationship between small host, schistosome parasite and human host was somewhat stabilized, and infection rates were low. Snail populations increased during the rainy season, when agriculture was possible, which provided the contact between man and parasites. During dry periods, however, there was a lull in infection. With the stabilization of water resource systems through the development of reservoirs and perennial irrigation schemes, the habitats for snails were vastly extended, and they also had a prolonged breeding phase which substantially increased their population. Furthermore, it provided more human contacts with parasites, which not only raised infection rates but also greatly increased worm load per man. The incidence and extension of these diseases can be directly related to the proliferation of irrigation schemes, the stabilization of the aquatic biotope and subsequent ecological changes.

The characteristics of snail habitats, as described by Malek (1972), are the following:

> They breed in many different sites, the essential conditions being the presence of water, relatively solid surfaces for egg deposition, and some source of food. These conditions are met by a large variety of habitats: streams, irrigation canals, ponds, borrow-pits, flooded areas, lakes, water-cress fields, and rice fields. Thus in general they inhabit shallow waters with organic content, moderate light penetration, little turbidity, a muddy substratum rich in organic matter, submergent or emergent aquatic vegetation, and abundant micro-flora.

Thus, water resources developments, especially improvements for hydropower, irrigation or fishing industry, are most likely to favour increased propagation and spread of these snails (World Bank, 1974).

The relationship between water developments and increase in schistosomiasis has been conclusively demonstrated in several countries of the world. In Egypt, the replacement of simple primitive irrigation with perennial irrigation has caused a high incidence of both *Schistosoma mansoni* and *S. haematobium*. Where basin irrigation is still practiced, the incidence is much less. Infection rates in four selected areas, within 3 years of introduction of perennial irrigation, rose from 10 to 44%, 7 to 50%, 11 to 64% and 2 to 75%. The life expectancy of males and females in heavily infected areas is estimated to be 27 and 25 years respectively. In Sudan, with the introduction of perennial irrigation to 900,000 acres under the Gezira Scheme, the incidence of blood fluke rose greatly. It also increased the incidence of flukes in cattle and sheep. In Kenya, the Lake Victoria is hyperendemic for schistosomiasis. *S. mansoni* infection in school children is up to 100% in areas associated with irrigation schemes. In Transvaal, South Africa, the *S. mansoni* infection rate in European farms was 68.5% compared with only 33.5% in the reserves, because the former had irrigation. Similarly, in the Far East, irrigation has not only increased schistosomiasis, but also diseases like liver fluke infections, eosinophilic meningitis and Bancroftian filariasis (Biswas and Biswas, 1975).

Constant availability of a large quantity of water in reservoirs and canals is also conducive to the breeding of mosquitos, which act as intermediate host for diseases like malaria, Bancroftian filariasis, yellow fever or arbovirus encephalitides. Currently it is estimated that over 200 million people are infected with malaria in the tropics and sub-tropics and another 250 million are infected with Bancroftian filariasis (UNEP, 1977). Similarly, plant growths around water bodies provide a suitable habitat for the tsetse fly to transmit trypanosomiasis to human beings and domestic animals.

In contrast to the diseases discussed above, water developments tend to reduce the incidence of onchocerciasis. The intermediate host, simulum fly, tends to breed in fast-flowing waters, which are often drowned following the construction of dams. Thus, the construction of the Volta Dam destroyed the breeding ground of simulum fly that existed upstream. However, adequate measures should be taken to ensure that new breeding places do not develop, especially in the fast-flowing waters near spillways.

Many cases can be cited in developing countries of Africa, Asia and Latin America where society has had to pay heavy prices for water development schemes in terms of the overall health of the region as well as through ecological deterioration. Thus, irrigation developments do not automatically and necessarily bring unmitigated benefits to mankind: they can, and do, extract high costs as well. What is necessary is a determined attempt to minimize the costs and maximize the benefits of such developments on a long-term sustaining basis. This can only be done if ecological and environmental principles are explicitly considered in the overall planning process right from the very beginning.

Aquatic weeds also can be the result of water resources development, especially in the tropics and semi-tropics. Serious problems of weed growth have been observed at Aswan, Kariba (Zambia and Rhodesia), Nam Pong (Thailand) and Brokopondo (Surinam). Unless adequate preventive measures are taken, growth of aquatic weed can be very fast. Thus, *Eichhornia crassipes*, commonly known as water hyacinth, covered an area of about

50 km² in Lake Brokopondo within the short period of February-December 1964. In little over 2 years, by April 1966, it had covered more than 50% of the surface of the reservoir, an area of about 410 km². Similarly, in Egypt, weeds were not a problem till 1964. However, in 1965, water hyacinth started to spread prolifically in the majority of drains and many canals in Middle Egypt and the Delta area. By the beginning of the spring of 1975, various types of aquatic weeds, sometimes mixed with dense algae, had invaded more than 80% of all the watercourses and a great part of the Nile itself (Kamel, 1977). Experience in the Congo Basin has been somewhat similar. Between 1952, when the weeds were first observed, and 1955, they spread a distance of some 1600 km, covering large areas of the Congo River.

In terms of water availability, and efficiency of water use, weeds are a great nuisance. Loss of water occurs due to two principal reasons. Firstly, a large amount of water is necessary in the canals for flow augmentation in order to ensure adequate quantity of water is available in the lower reaches. Secondly, water losses are greatly enhanced by evapotranspiration from the weeds. These two factors often account for a tremendous amount of water loss. Thus, at Aswan, it has been estimated that 2.875 billion m³ of water is lost per yr due to the above two factors alone. A better perspective can be obtained, if it is considered that at present prices, 2.875 billion m³ of annual over-year storage on the upper reaches of the Nile at Aswan will cost some $216 million, which is not an insignificant figure (Kamel, 1977). In addition to water loss, there are other direct benefits which accrue from the control of aquatic weeds. Among these are:

significant increase in the efficiency of operation of drainage networks;
improvement of water quality;
lowering of the level of the water table, and thus less drainage requirements;
improvement of navigation;
reduction in dredging and excavation;
reduction of incidence of malaria and schistosomiasis since weeds tend to support invertebrates such as mosquitoes and aquatic snails, which are vectors and intermediate hosts for disease-causing agents;
less problems with the operation and maintenance of pumping and hydroelectric stations; and
reduction in competition with fish for space and nutrients.

Control of aquatic weeds in the tropics and semi-tropics, especially after invasion, is a difficult and expensive task. Mechanized or manual clearing of weeds, especially in shallow waters, has been quite successful, but in deep waters it is not a very viable alternative. Weeds thus removed can be used to produce animal feed, biogas or manure. In certain countries, such as China, aquatic plants are specially cultivated as animal feed.

Chemical herbicides have been extensively used to control weeds. Thus, Egypt has a major programme for spraying 2,4-D using motor launches and boats in the River Nile and the northern lakes (Kamel, 1977). Chemical control is not very effective for submerged weeds. In addition, herbicides often pose a major environmental hazard to aquatic organisms, deteriorate water quality and their long-term effects on aquatic ecosystem and human health are little understood.

The third type of control is biological, wherein fish, snails or aquatic grasshoppers are introduced to control weeds. There is still much to be learnt concerning the use of biological controls. Naturally, the three control measures are not mutually exclusive; often they are used in various combinations for optimal weed control. The type of control measures to be used depends on various local situations like the type of weed, density of infestation, depth and width of the channel, time of application, water use pattern, proximity of crop area sensitive to herbicides, availability of material from local or foreign sources and availability of skilled manpower.

HUMAN SUB-SYSTEM

The impacts of water developments on the human sub-system could be direct or indirect, stemming from direct effects on physical and biological sub-systems. These impacts can either be beneficial or adverse.

Provision of potable water to the rural or urban population is undoubtedly a major benefit of water developments. It immediately reduces the health hazards significantly, and further contributes to other major direct and indirect benefits. Thus, it is not surprising that the UN Conference on Human Settlements considered the availability of potable water to all the population of the world a priority item, and recommended that such a development should be complete by 1990 (Biswas, M. R., 1977a). The recently convened UN Water Conference further re-endorsed the importance of this step (Biswas, M. R., 1977b).

Major beneficiaries of the availability of potable water will be the women of the developing world, who currently spend considerable time in carrying water and collecting firewood. According to the Economic Commission for Africa of the United Nations, 90% of all water and fuel is collected by women: men only contribute to 10% of this task (UNECA, 1975). Thus, rational water resources development and management will reduce the water collection journey, made mainly by women and children, who currently spend up to 5 hr every day collecting the family water requirements (White *et al.*, 1972). Table 3 shows that time spent in carrying water is a function of the distance of the source from the consumer, and also how it affects the total daily working time of water carriers (UN Water Conference, 1977). It shows that if the water source is about 4½ miles away, a woman would spend at least 3 hr a day carrying water or 50% of her daily working time. If this time can be freed by providing water closer to the residences, it can be used for learning or productive work.

Table 3. Time spent for water collection in Africa.

Distance between water source and consumer (miles)	Time spent in collecting water (hr)	% of average daily working time spent in collecting water
0.25	0.166	2.8
0.50	0.333	5.5
1.00	0.667	11.1
2.00	1.333	22.2
3.00	2.000	33.3
4.00	2.667	44.4
5.00	3.333	55.5
6.00	4.000	66.6
7.00	4.667	77.7
8.00	5.333	88.8
9.00	6.000	100.0

Source: UN Water Conference (1977).

Time and inconvenience are not the only disadvantages of a long water collection journey for the women of the developing countries: it extols other costs as well. It has been estimated that it takes up to 12% of daytime calorie needs of most carriers in non-dry areas and in drier areas and in mountainous regions, energy spent in collecting water and firewood may take up to 25% or more of the daytime calories (Cleave, 1974). Women are not traditionally the most well-nourished member of the family: the most nutritious food being normally reserved for the men, the breadwinners of the family (Biswas, M. R., 1978). Thus, elimination of the water collection journey for women, by providing potable water closer to home, has not only important implications in terms of reduced disease propagation (since contacts with disease vectors during long water collection journeys would be eliminated) but also in terms of nutrition, a fact often overlooked by planners and politicians.

All impacts on the human sub-system due to water developments, however, are not beneficial: there are many adverse impacts as well (Biswas and Biswas, 1976). Many of the effects mentioned earlier under the sections on physical and biological sub-systems also have impacts on the human sub-system. However, distinction could be made that such developments initially contribute to environmental and ecological changes, which in turn affect the human sub-system. Under the present section, only direct impacts on the human sub-system will be discussed.

Many of the major water development projects have also created other human problems, especially in terms of displacement of local inhabitants. Thus, the Volta Dam in Ghana has inundated an area of about 3275 square miles, and the resulting lake has a shoreline of over 4000 miles. As a result of this development, some 78,000 people and more than 170,000 domestic animals had to be evacuated from over 700 towns and villages of different sizes. Eventually, 52 new settlements were developed to house 69,149 people from 12,789 families (Jones and Rogers, 1976). This was a major social problem since a large number of people coming from small villages (600 of the 700 original villages has less than 100 people, and only one had a population of over 4000), and having different ethnic backgrounds, languages, traditions, religions, social values and cultures, had to be resettled into only 52 locations. The complex emotional relationships between the different tribes and their lands were not properly understood. There were many who found it very hard to make a clean break with their ancestral roots, by leaving their gods, shrines and graves of ancestors. The development of a socially cohesive and integrated community, having a viable institutional infrastructure, became hard to achieve.

The economic stability of the settlers depended on agricultural products from family farming plots. Unfortunately land clearing schemes did not progress on schedule, and in some cases cleared areas were not ready for farming when the settlers arrived. The World Food Programme had to step in to avoid a major catastrophe (Biswas, 1977).

Similarly, the Kariba Dam on the Zambesi (Zambia and Rhodesia) displaced approximately 57,000 Tonga tribesmen, who had to pay a major price for this progress. Technology transfer at that level was a major problem, since many of the planners were from outside Africa. The resettlement programme for the Tonga tribesmen left much to be desired; not only did they suffer great cultural shocks when being thrust into communities as different from their own as theirs from Great Britain, but also it took 2 years to clear sufficient land to meet their subsistence needs. The government had to step in to avert famine and very serious hardships and, ironically, this well-intentioned step became one of the most destructive parts of the process. The food distribution centres also became transmission sites for the dreaded sleeping sickness disease.

Similar results from water development projects have, unfortunately, not been unique. Approximately 100,000 people had to be relocated due to the Aswan High Dam without sufficient planning, and the World Food Programme had to rush in famine relief for the Nubians. Other examples of lakes and populations displaced are the following: Lake Kainji in Nigeria—42,000; Keban Dam in Turkey—30,000; Sarafore Reservoir on the Volga—23,000, and Ubolratana Dam in Thailand—30,000 (UNEP, 1977). In the United States, the Tennessee Valley Authority had to relocate 12,000 families.

Resettlement of population due to water development projects in many developing countries has not been a satisfactory experience. Inadequate planning, insufficient budget, incomplete execution of plans and little appreciation of the problems of technology transfer have all contributed to the failure of plans. The fact that many of the people to be resettled were rural and illiterate, and thus had very little political power, did not help either. The direct beneficiaries of the projects were often the educated elites, who are in power, whereas the direct social costs were mostly attributable to the rural poor. Thus, in most cases, the nature of the beneficiaries, as distinct from the nature of the benefits accruing from the development projects, is seldom emphasized (Biswas, 1973). Yet, the nature of the beneficiaries, from the viewpoints of regional development or redistribution of income, is undoubtedly a major planning parameter.

CONCLUSIONS

There is no doubt that the primary effects of the vast majority of water development projects around the world have been beneficial. Equally, however, there is no doubt that many of these development projects have contributed to unanticipated adverse secondary effects, some of which could have been eliminated and others reduced in magnitude by appropriate planning process. Furthermore, there appears to be a considerable difference of opinions on criteria and techniques by which successes or failures of projects can be judged. Hence, it is not exactly unusual to find a major water development project hailed as a technological triumph by engineers, welcomed as a success in terms of economic efficiency and regional income distribution by economists, but seriously questioned as to its desirability by environmentalists and sociologists. Such an anomalous situation often indicates the lack of adequate interdisciplinary interactions during the planning process, which means the objective functions that are being maximized by different groups are not the same. Lack of public participation during the planning and construction phases further complicates the situation.

The addition of environmental quality in recent years to the other two traditionally accepted objectives of water resources development—economic efficiency and regional income redistribution—has made the planning process more complex than ever before. Inclusion of environmental quality as an objective of development recognizes the fact that the welfare of the society has other dimensions besides economics, and hence the real question is not whether environmental quality should be considered as a planning objective, but rather how it should be incorporated objectively within the planning framework.

Existing analytical techniques available for making planning decisions cannot effectively cope with the social, ecological and environmental concerns. To give just one example, economic analyses in terms of marginal benefit-cost consideration cannot handle these types of complex problems. Damages to the environment caused by the construction of a dam, whether to the beauty of a canyon or the countryside, or to the overall ecology, cannot be analysed by the fine tuning of marginalism. Neither can this approach be successfully used where benefits are short-run and quantifiable while the costs are long-run and often unknown and unquantifiable (Biswas and Coomber, 1973). Such analyses often involve the question of choice or value judgement. The cost of upgrading the quality of water, air or land is measurable, but the benefits accrued by improving an additional unit of water, air or land quality is immeasurable, and hence in the realm of values. Such situations, however, are not unique: like many other social choices, decisions and value judgements have to be made through the political process.

Finally, planning is for the people, and planners must give adequate emphasis to the social and environmental consequences stemming from water development projects. Technical and economic feasibility studies are needed, but equally necessary are social and environmental feasibility studies. Without such analyses, public understanding and acceptance of the programme, an important parameter to judge the success of water development projects, may not be complete. Planners and engineers must learn from past mistakes committed, and should not make similar mistakes all over again. The planning process should become more sensitive to social and environmental problems, since long-term sustaining developments can only take place within the framework of appropriate environmental guidelines: otherwise the overall strategy of development will be self-defeating. Harmony can come only with integrated planning but discord is comparatively easy to produce.

REFERENCES

Abl Atta, A. Country Speech of Egypt to the UN Water Conference, Mar del Plata, Argentina, (1977).

Biswas, Asit K. *History of Hydrology*, North-Holland Publishing Co., Amsterdam, (1972) 336 pp.

Biswas, Asit K. Socio-economic considerations in water resources planning, *Water Resour. Bull.*, 9 (4), 746-754 (1973).

Biswas, Asit K. Environmental implications of energy development, in *Engineering Issues*, American Society of Civil Engineers, 103 (EI 1), 49-59 (1977).

Biswas, Asit K. Loss of productive soil, *Int. J. Environ. Stud.*, 12, 1-9 (1978).

Biswas, Asit K. Water: A perspective on global issues and politics, *J. Water Resour.* Plann. Manage. Div., Am. Soc. Civ. Engrs (To be published) (1978).

Biswas, Asit K. and Biswas, Margaret R. Environmental impacts of increasing world's food production, *Agric. Environ.*, 2, 291-309 (1975).

Biswas, Asit K. and Biswas, Margaret R. Hydro-power and the environment. *Water Pwr Dam Constr.*, 28, 40-43 (1976).

Biswas, Asit K. and Biswas, Maragret R. Food production and environment, in *Food, Climate and Man*, Biswas, A. K. and Biswas, M. R. (eds) John Wiley, New York, (1978).

Biswas, Asit K. and Coomber, N. H. *Evaluation of Environmental Intangibles*, Genera Press, Bronxville, (1973).

Biswas, Asit K. and Durie, Robert W. Sociological aspects of water development, *Water Resour. Bull.*, 7, 1137-1143 (1971).

Biswas, Margaret R. Habitat in retrospect, *Int. J. Environ. Stud.*, (1977a).

Biswas, Margaret R. UN water conference: a perspective, *Water Supply & Management*, **1**, 255-272 (1977b).

Biswas, Margaret R. Nutrition and development, *Int. J. Environ. Stud.*, (1978).

Bradley, D. J. Water supplies: The consequences of change, in *Human Rights in Health*, CIBA Foundation Symposium No. 23, Associated Scientific Publishers, Amsterdam, (1974).

Cleave, J. H. *African Farmers: Labour Use in the Development of Smallhold Agriculture*, Praeger Publishers, New York, (1974).

Feachem, R. The rational allocation of water resources for the domestic needs of rural communities of developing countries, *Proceedings, 2nd Congress*, International Water Resources Association, New York, (1975) pp. 539-546.

Hafez, M. and Shenouda, W. K. The environmental impacts of the Aswan High Dam, in *Water Development and Management*, Biswas, Asit K. (ed.) Pergamon Press, Oxford, (1978).

Jones, J. O. and Rogers, P. *Human Ecology and Development of Settlements*, Plenum Press, New York, (1976) pp. 23-31.

Kamel, J. Aquatic weed problems in Egypt, in *Water Development and Management*, Biswas, Asit K. (ed.) Pergamon Press, Oxford, (1978).

Muller, R. Dracunculus and Dracunculiasis, in *Advances in Parasitology*, Dawes, B. (ed.) Academic Press, New York, (1971).

Malek, E. A. Snail ecology and man-made habitats, in *Schistosomiasis*, Muller, M. J. (ed.) Tulane University, New Orleans, (1972).

Ongyweny, G. S. Problems of soil erosion and sedimentation in selected water catchment areas in Kenya with special reference to the Tana River, in *Water Development and Management*, Biswas, Asit K. (ed.) Pergamon Press, Oxford, (1978).

Rothe, J. P. Summary: geophysics report, in *Man-made Lakes: Their Problems and Environmental Effects*, Ackermann, W. C., White, G. F. and Worthington, E. B. (eds) Monograph No. 17, American Geophysical Union, Washington DC, (1973).

UN Economic Commission for Africa, *Women of Africa Today and Tomorrow*, UN Economic Commission for Africa, Addis Ababa, (1975).

UN Economic and Social Council, Problem of water resources development in Africa, in *Water Development and Management*, Biswas, Asit K. (ed.) Pergamon Press, Oxford, (1978).

UN Environment Programme, Environmental issues in river basin development, in *Water Development and Management*, Biswas, Asit K. (ed.) Pergamon Press, Oxford, (1978).

UN Water Conference *Water, Women and Development*, UN Water Conference, E/CONF. 70/A. 19. Mar del Plata, Argentina, (1977) 22 pp.

White, G. F., Bradley, D. J. and Emurwon, P. *Drawers of Water: Domestic Water Use in Africa*. University of Chicago Press, Chicago, (1972).

World Bank, *Environmental Health and Human Ecologic Considerations in Economic Development Projects*, World Bank, Washington DC, (1974) pp. 50-52.

Planning and Management of Rural Water Development

"To be successful, planned irrigation technology transfer must include not only the hardware but also the software of services institutions and attitudes."

Ian Carruthers

Water Supply & Management, Vol. 2, pp. 301-308.
© Pergamon Press Ltd., 1978. Printed in Great Britain.

0364-7714/78/0801-0301$02.00/0

Contentious Issues in Planning Irrigation Schemes

IAN CARRUTHERS

This paper is a personal statement of some of the impressions and ideas gained in recent practical research, advisory and planning work in the irrigation field in several developing countries. It is difficult, sometimes impossible, to sustain by reference to empirical evidence or theory some of my observations. Nevertheless, I venture to present the main arguments and ideas, many of which are testable, because several of the contentions, if valid, will be of importance to the planning process for irrigation development. My ideological base stems essentially from neo-classical positive economics.[1]

INCREASED POTENTIAL

Advances in the technological aspects of agricultural production and in engineering aspects of project construction and operation have increased the prospects of profitable irrigation. Whilst the potential has increased, the little information on performance suggests that the gap between potential and realised benefits has, in fact, increased. Nevertheless, the main motivation for continued planning of irrigation projects is the vision of the new higher water response function and thus the prospect of a more productive agricultural system.

There are several possible reasons for the gap between potential and realized benefits. Defects may occur at the planning, implementation and operation phase or at various combinations of these activities. I intend to concentrate upon the former phase although this does not imply that it is considered the most important area of defect.

In the case of most irrigation schemes the planning procedure is becoming a modelling process that is quite divorced from reality. Thus, although the apparent increasing sophistication of the economic and engineering analytical procedures in, for example, designs, appraisals and critical path routines, the most recent investments are, at best, performing no better than earlier irrigation projects.

The proven (or more often, rumoured) existence of low productivity in existing schemes is sometimes put down to poor planning leading to misallocated resources. Engineers, for example, complain of too little time-series hydrological data and react by building elaborate simulation models or insuring against failure by adopting large safety factors. Economists have reacted by developing elaborate analytical procedures of cost-benefit assessment—a topic to which I will return later.

The basic thesis of this paper is not so much that the planning procedures used by any particular party to the process are defective in themselves but that participants do not integrate their professional activities according to an agreed conceptual understanding of the problems; that the criteria adopted at various stages in the planning process are not consistent; that the lessons to be gained from operating experience are denied; and finally that technological solutions cannot help overcome fundamental institutional problems.

INTEREST GROUPS PROMOTING IRRIGATION

Figure 1 sets out the main interest groups (pressure groups?) involved in irrigation. Each group has its own functional preoccupation. Thus agronomists are concerned with crop yield or the returns to land from modern developments which facilitate multiple cropping. Engineers seek to satisfy a vision through new diversion structures whereas planners and administrators, being generally followers of Wittfogel (1959), look to the gains from control. Aid donors and politicians have a fairly close coincidence of interests although the politician usually has a very short-term view. It always strikes me as ironic that we place responsibility for curbing our "defective telescopic faculty" for the future, in the hands of individuals whose prime interests seldom exceed 5 years. Irrigation and water supply satisfy many of the criteria of aid donors being readily acceptable and apparently "non-political" forms of donation and, in the case of the UK, facilitating a continued exploitation of our technological skills in this area.

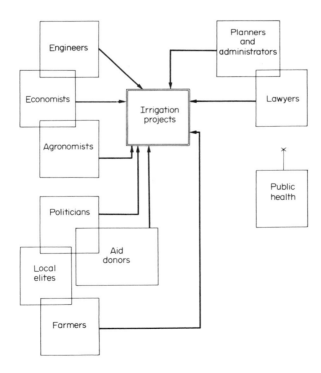

Fig. 1. Irrigation planning interest groups.

Good irrigation plans can cover all the trendy elements in the current development literature, being rural, serving income redistribution, basic needs, enhancing food surplus, creating employment and incorporating appropriate technology and sound ecological principles for environmental protection. In the event most schemes appear to create subsidized income elites; contribute to food production only at high cost; facilitate preconditions for inappropriate mechanization and thus a disappointing employment creation record; and they lead to various aspects of environmental degradation. Public health considerations are typically ignored (see the paper by Feachem in this publication).

ECONOMIC PREOCCUPATIONS

Economists involved in irrigation planning have been concerned with problems of social valuation of inputs and outputs, of coping with differences in their timing, of assessing the associated risks and most recently with questions related to the incidence of costs and benefits.

It is my contention, that whilst these issues are central to the development of worthwhile workable plans, the form of the economic intervention has generally been inappropriate and ineffective.

The main contribution of economists to irrigation planning has been to develop a public view of resource disposition and output assessment. In developing countries, markets for factors of production and products are so distorted by a variety of influences (mainly Government interventions) that economists have constructed a shadow world where prices reflect the opportunity cost and they have built up methods of assessment of the merit of alternative plans on the basis of shadow prices (Little and Mirrlees, 1974; Squire and Van der Tak, 1975). In doing so they have extended an area of theory (welfare economics) into the practical world and extended it further than other branches of economic theory that are equally relevant to project planning. For example, the conceptual insights stemming from production functions and input-output analysis, are essential for planning agricultural production programmes and whilst there is a considerable literature on the theory of these topics there are no *manuals* comparable to those advocating shadow pricing techniques.

The practical implication of this development has become a cause for concern since the procedures became more elaborate, since rival or alternative manuals were published and since the application has been inconsistent. Most decision makers and many economists simply fail to understand the advocated procedures, particularly since they were "improved" by incorporating (by weighting procedures) objectives other than economic efficiency into a single measure of project worth. Various schools of thought have developed in this field with few real differences in the practical implications but the differences which do exist are very confusing when making comparisons between projects appraised by alternative methods.[2]

Although economists have, in many instances, systematically applied shadow pricing at the appraisal stage, it is still true to say that engineers have been little influenced by the concept in resolving design issues. Contractors are unimpressed when the shadow wage is half the money wage if imported machinery can do the job cost-effectively given an over-valued exchange rate. In addition, even economists, if wearing their Treasury hat, find the need to provide labour subsidies more than the budget can bear. Hence my contention that application of these insights is inconsistent among the various participants in irrigation development.

I do not wish to deal at length with the (important) issues of timing and risk assessment. It is sufficient to say that in relation to timing, economists divide into two main opposite schools. One stresses (high, usually) social opportunity cost rates and one (low, usually) social time preference rate, with the latter, on balance, gaining the edge with academics and the former with practitioners. The choice of rate is not unimportant because it may influence the degree of capital intensity or even the choice of technology (e.g. groundwater development vs surface storage). Assessment of risk is important, particularly on the agricultural output side which is subject to undue economic and biological risk. Unfortunately, the agricultural planning profession has of late spent more energies, to little real effect, upon shadow pricing procedures than on a study of the nature and importance of uncertainty in the rural sector.

Economists, in emphasizing the public view, in a form and language that carries great weight, have helped to bring about a neglect of financial criteria. The stresses upon the recurrent budget of many Governments are creating considerable inefficiency. However, evidence is accruing that financial availability is once more becoming an effective decision criteria, although it is not always applied in a desirable form.

FARMER INVOLVEMENT

The first draft of Fig. 1 excluded the farmers, although I have been drawing this diagram, or something like it, for a decade. Why is this? Could there lie behind this admission, which on reflection reveals a widespread attitude, a partial explanation for poor performance of plans.

It is easy to understand why farmers have been by-passed in the past. Firstly, agricultural information is often held in low regard by planners. It is only relatively recently that professional agriculturalists have been involved in irrigation planning and still their role is limited to providing the model cropping patterns which form the basis for irrigation design and which may, or may not, be adopted by farmers. If professional agriculturalists were excluded then it is to be expected that farmers would be also. Secondly, many irrigation projects were for "empty" areas or for farmers totally new to irrigation. Thirdly, as farmers are a relatively large and heterogeneous group, a few representative farmers might be hard to identify. Fourthly, the generally low level of education does not facilitate effective communication with planners. By and large, it is my experience that most planners have a paternalistic view of their role and an unhealthy regard for the possible value of farmer participation in the planning process. Failure to appreciate and be sensitive to the socio-political realities of the social environment into which irrigation technology is to be introduced is a sure recipe for problems later. Agriculture has special problems not encountered in industry and the way in which these problems influence decision making at the farm level is best understood by farmers.

INCOME REDISTRIBUTION

It is a recent realization of economists that the equity question cannot be regarded as a second phase problem to be handled by subsidies or taxes once value added has been maximized. For a variety of reasons, the second phase is never satisfactorily completed, even by the declared criteria of those controlling the redistribution policy instruments. The "trickle down" effect of the massive public investments of the 1950s and 1960s has been seen to be very aptly described as a trickle.

There are two basic approaches to incorporating income redistribution goals (and other objectives, e.g. regional development) into project plans. Alternatives can be assessed by reference to independent criteria indicating their value according to each objective and these can be scanned, a subjective weighting given to each outcome and choice made. Alternatively, multiple objectives can be incorporated into a single index with predetermined weightings. This latter procedure termed social cost-benefit analysis is presently the most favoured by OECD, UNIDO, latterly the World Bank and several bilateral aid agencies. This is, in my view, a misdirection of effort.[3] There are several reasons for this trend but the most telling, attributed to Ian Little, one of the foremost authors and advocates of this form of social cost-benefit analysis is that it is a means of "smuggling in" income distribution considerations.

I contend that this procedure is doomed to fail because the seeds of its own failure will be stimulated to growth with every modicum of success. It may be possible to bemuse the authorities for a time but if this policy instrument really works and is perceived to threaten the existing interests of the elite decision-making group, then these analyses will be ignored (as they have been ignored so often for big projects in the West). There is already a powerful tool for achieving income redistribution and that is taxation. Taxation is well known to be largely a failure in LDC's and for the same basic reasons that cause this to occur, we can also predict that social cost-benefit analysis will fail.

AUTOMATE TO BY-PASS MANAGEMENT BOTTLENECKS

Much of the technology used on new irrigation projects has been devised to cope with essentially different problems of developed countries but, although there may be many other reasons for the inappropriateness of direct technology transfer (Vandenberghe, 1977), it finds uses in Third World countries to by-pass the apparently intractable management problems which arise either in the supply of water, or in its on-farm use. Such an approach is doomed to fail because the contrasting resource endowment situation of developed countries generally produces technologically inappropriate solutions for Third World conditions. In addition, modern "Western" technology creates new management problems which require higher-level skills (FAO, 1974) but these problems appear no less amenable to solution. Indeed, automation may create different maintenance problems which are beyond the capacity of the country to solve. Furthermore, parts of the package necessary to assure success may be unknown. For example, the levels of response to various levels of water inputs at different stages of plant growth. Technology may assist countries and farmers to achieve their declared objectives but it has no magic properties to speed the process and there is always the risk that it is diverting attention from more fundamental institutional developments. Sometimes the desire for speed or the terms of aid can also lead to inappropriate technical solutions.

EX-POST EVALUATION

The lessons of operating experience are very largely ignored in planning. The design of dams, wells and structures is a specialized task and the practitioners seldom have either operating experience or access to analytical studies of factors leading to success or failure in previous projects. The planning process with the close consultant-client-contractor relationship and very limited public discussion of either objectives and means does not help.

Ex-post evaluation should be a systematic review procedure. There is the danger of an evaluation study being a vague, historical or descriptive treatise, of little value for pre-scription and containing few concrete lessons. A major methodological issue inhibiting a systematic approach relates to choice of criteria or tests of preferredness. Obvious criteria will be of a technical, economic and financial nature but other goals may be set concerned with employment, regional impact, nutrition and self-sufficiency which will also require tests of achievement. A decade ago, economic efficiency was regarded as a valid proxy measure for social welfare goals. Its main defect arose from the need to give a premium to savings and a higher priority to individuals, groups or regions by-passed by the economic growth process. This has led to the advocacy of more complex procedures for assessing the impact of alternative projects upon inter-temporal and inter-personal welfare. Criteria set in relation to various goals are not inherently equal. Whilst technical feasibility may be considered a necessary condition for development, overriding all other criteria, various standards of technical performance above some minimum level may be optimal. Evaluation studies should examine several aspects of technical performance. The relative weight given in evaluation to technical, economic, financial, legal, administrative and other aspects of project performance in order to establish the degree of success cannot be predetermined, but they are weighted implicitly or explicitly in the design and appraisal stages.

The neglect of ex-post evaluation is a major reason for the repetition of planning mistakes, as well as poor operating performance. However, I do not anticipate much change in this situation because rigorous evaluation is generally not in the short-term interest of the operating authorities or the aid donors (Carruthers and Clayton, 1977).

STUDY OF INSTITUTIONS

More ex-post evaluation by interdisciplinary groups would help us to understand *why* performance is poor. There is one area which is almost totally neglected, and that is a study of the institutions supporting and benefiting from irrigation. By institutions I refer to the norms, rules of conduct and generally accepted ways of doing things. Institutions may be social, political or economic. In irrigation planning such aspects are neglected. There is very little analysis of *why* prospects are not realized and not much written in the economic field, to my knowledge, on the methodology of such analysis. Such studies are the clear prerogative of sociologists, but my own experience suggests to me that my engineering colleagues' general prejudice against their participation unfortunately has some foundation in fact. I would emphasize that, to be successful, planned irrigation technology transfer must include not only the hardware but also the software of services, institutions and attitudes. Some authors contend that the technology adopted, largely reflects the interests of those holding power in society (e.g. politicians, bureaucrats, urban consumers, large landowners) and technology appropriate to the majority may be excluded (Stewart, 1977). Ruttan (1977) contends that technical change in agriculture is endogenously generated but that institutional change is not occurring to keep up with the technical potential. He states that:

> (the) developing world is still trying to cope with the debris of non-viable institutional innovations: with extension services with no capacity to extend knowledge or little knowledge to extend; cooperatives that serve to channel resources to village elites; price stabilisation policies that have the effect of amplifying commodity price fluctuations; and rural development programmes that are incapable of expanding the resources available to rural people.
>
> . . . unless social science research can generate new knowledge leading to viable institutional innovation and more effective institutional performance, the potential productivity growth made possible by scientific and technical innovation will be under utilised.

I would concur with this perspective. My experience of planning water use in agriculture suggests that political economy coupled with scientific insight is the only suitable framework for evaluation of development that is likely to lead to an improved performance in the vital rural sector.

It can be concluded that in the planning process which has evolved over the last two decades there has been great emphasis upon methodology and that the intellectual inputs, if not the outputs, are most impressive. However, there has been a relative neglect of the data supply to service this methodology. Recent efforts to assemble the basic technical information in many cases compare unfavourably with many similar studies 100 years or so ago.[4] It may be that the potential for irrigation is not being realized largely because of deficiency in the operating policies but I would argue that to some extent the planning process lacks content in science and political economy and it is imbalanced in being preoccupied with certain issues that are not of central importance to irrigation's success.

NOTES

[1] Marxist analysis offers fascinating insights, but to date, I must admit insufficient theoretical background either to absorb them in some systematic way or to view my experience from that perspective. Furthermore, the practical policy implications of Marxist analysis of agricultural, as opposed to urban, sector problems as presented in the literature of development studies appears to be particularly deficient.

[2] For example some methods use domestic currency, some foreign exchange as unit of account. However, one suspects, and there is evidence to support this, that in practice, most methods would produce very similar technical solutions, optimum scale and timing, and ranking.

[3] For a complete presentation of this position, see the review article by the author in *ODI Review*, **2** (1977).

[4] For an early and fine example of the nineteenth century penchant for fact collection and analysis, see reports of the 131 specialists that accompanied Napoleon into Egypt 1778-1801. Guemard, G. *Histoire et bibliographie critique de la Commission des Sciences et Arts et de l'Institut d'Egypte,* Le Caire chez l'Auteur, (1936). Quoted by A. Zahlan. UNECWA Technology Transfer Conference, Beirut, October 1977.

REFERENCES

Carruthers, I. D. Applied project appraisal—the state of the art, *ODI Review,* **2**, 12-28 (1977).

Carruthers, I. D. and Clayton, E. S. Ex-post evaluation of agricultural projects—its implication for planning, *J. Agric. Econ.* **XXVIII** (3), (1977).

FAO, *Studies in technological forecasting*, ECA: 19/74 (10), Rome, (1974).

Little, I. M. D. and Mirrlees, J. *Project Appraisal and Planning for Less Developed Countries,* Heinemann, London, (1974).

Ruttan, V. R. Induced innovation and agricultural development, *Food Policy*, 2(3), 196-216 (1977).

Squire, L. and Vand der Tak, H. G. *Economic Analysis of Projects,* Tomas Hopkins for World Bank, Washington, (1975).

Stewart, F. Technology and underdevelopment, *ODI Review*, 1, 92-105 (1977).

Vandenberghe, P. The technology came from abroad. *Ceres*, (January/February 1977).

Wittfogel, K. A. *Oriental Despotism*, Yale University Press, (1957).

Water Supply & Management, Vol. 2, pp. 309-332.
© Pergamon Press Ltd., 1978. Printed in Great Britain.

0364-7714/78/0801-0309$02.00/0

The Management and Operation of Irrigation Schemes in Less Developed Countries

ANTHONY BOTTRALL

This paper starts from the generally agreed proposition that the performance of most irrigation schemes in the developing world has been very disappointing. Planners' targets are rarely met: the overall productivity of water is much lower than might be expected and, especially on large surface-water delivery systems, the pattern of its distribution is often extremely inequitable, with farmers in the head-reaches receiving far more than those at the tail, whose supplies (if they get any at all) tend to be sparse and unreliable. The main thesis of the paper is that a very significant part of this poor performance (though by no means all of it) can be attributed to deficiencies in "management", both in the delivery of water to the farm and in its use on the farm, and that major social and economic benefits can be obtained from devising and implementing policies and procedures designed to combat these deficiencies. The remedies cost little in purely financial terms, though it would be foolish to pretend that they are capable of effective implementation without substantial administrative inputs in the form of research and training programmes or without a high degree of political commitment on the part of the governments of the countries concerned.

Different kinds of management problems tend to be associated with different types of irrigation project. The main emphasis in this paper is on large publicly-operated schemes in which surface-water is distributed by gravity flow. This is partly because schemes of this kind are the most common source of irrigation water in most parts of the developing world; partly because a particularly large proportion of their problems can often be attributed to deficiencies in "man-management" and it is this aspect of irrigation management (as opposed to the more technical aspects) which has been most conspicuously neglected, by governments, donor agencies and researchers alike. But before the final section of the paper on research and training priorities, reference is also made to the management problems which are commonly encountered in two other contexts: (a) in areas supplied by small "indigenous" surface water systems; these typically employ simple technology and are operated by farmers themselves with little or no assistance from government; and (b) in areas dependent wholly or partly on groundwater extraction; these may involve the use of a wide range of technologies with different degrees of sophistication.

If the paper were to be comprehensive, reference would also have to be made to the management problems associated with other relatively high-technology methods of irrigation, both for water extraction (e.g. large surface pumps) and water application (e.g. sprinkler and trickle irrigation). But they appear to have no particularly distinctive problems of man-management; most of them are more of a technical nature (lack of adequate maintenance and repair facilities; difficulties in obtaining imported spare parts, etc.). Besides, sprinkler and trickle irrigation are still very rarely used in most less developed countries, except for a few oil-rich countries (e.g. Libya) and on some commercial estates. So, in the interests of brevity, they are not discussed further here.

LARGE PUBLICLY-OPERATED SURFACE SYSTEMS

Why are management problems—and particularly man-management problems—so frequently encountered on large publicly-operated surface systems? Most of the reasons appear to be somehow associated with the following five factors:

(a) Scale

"Large" irrigation projects, as defined here, may range in size from something as small as the Mwea project in Kenya (about 5000 ha) to something as large as a Command Area Development project in India (about 250,000 ha) or even the Gezira scheme in Sudan (about 800,000 ha); but they are all discrete management units, usually dependent on a single major source of water supply, which are operated by government or para-statal agencies. The larger the scale, the longer the distances and, with them, the greater the potential problems of communication and information. These are not problems peculiar to irrigation projects (they can be found on agricultural development projects of other kinds) but they are often more difficult to avoid on irrigation projects, where the area commanded by a single dam or reservoir, which may necessarily be large, determines the area which has to be managed as a single unit. Moreover, on irrigation projects the importance of the activity of allocating water to a large number of independent users (the right quantity, in the right place, at the right time) implies a much greater *need* for good communications and accurate information, on a regular basis, than on other kinds of agricultural projects or programmes.

(b) Indivisibility

This is linked to the scale factor: the problems associated with it (which are mainly in the initial years of a project's development) increase with the project's size. When the construction of a new dam or reservoir has been completed, the whole of the commanded area will be supplied with water within a very short space of time, and within that short time a complete new management apparatus will have to be brought into operation. The difficulties entailed by this, especially in countries where management capacity is a scarce resource are obvious. And the need for a "management-intensive" approach during the initial period of irrigation development is compounded by the planners' requirements for rapid economic and financial returns to the very large capital investments incurred. Such sudden heavy demands on management capacity are much more easily avoidable on other agricultural projects or programmes, where investment tends to be relatively divisible.

The same is true of irrigation development which is dependent on wells or other smaller-scale investments. This is not the place to argue whether or not more attention should be paid to the development of smaller irrigation projects at the expense of larger ones. There is no disagreement with Levine's observations that, although "there are undoubtedly many large projects which can be justified, . . . opportunities for . . . increasing irrigation capabilities through the alternatives of smaller projects have not been explored adequately" (Levine, 1977). But this is essentially an issue for the planners (though in reaching their decisions they should take the probable management implications into account much more than they usually do. Once a project has been completed, managers can do no more than operate what exists as well as they are able—and this may sometimes mean trying to make the best of a bad (planning) job.

(c) Inflexibility

Large surface systems are capable of different degrees of flexibility in their operation, depending on their technical design characteristics (whether they are with or without storage; how many and what kind of control structures exist within the distribution system), but they can never be as flexible in matching the pattern of water supplies to the demands of the individual farmer as—to take an extreme example—a privately-operated tubewell. Even so-called "on-demand" systems (such as can be found in the USA) will require farmers to "queue" for their water at times of peak requirements—and the flexibility they provide can only be obtained at a high cost. So, where water is a scarce resource—as it is on most irrigation projects—management staff are faced with one of two problems: either with trying to achieve an optimal match between a (more or less) inflexible water supply and the complex demand pattern which may be produced if farmers are allowed to grow their crops on a free choice basis—a situation calling for an excellent two-way information system and high levels of computing skill—or with trying to control demand, by establishing control over farmers' choices of cropping patterns and cultivation schedules, in such a way that it closely matches the inflexible pattern of water supplies—which calls for skill in farm management planning and the authority and/or powers of persuasion to convince farmers of the advantages of falling in with the prescribed plans. Although the demands placed on management skills are different in each case, they are both of a high order—much higher than most planners or policymakers generally recognize. Over and above the management (and economic) implications of choosing one approach rather than the other are certain quasi-political or ideological implications: Approach A could be typified as "liberal", Approach B as authoritarian and interventionist. In fact, when planners decide which approach to adopt in a particular locality, their decision rarely seems to have been based on a conscious choice between alternatives and it is doubtful whether many of them realize the full implications of their decision. For more on the present haphazard process whereby organizational and institutional "choices" are made, see below.

(d) Need for inter-departmental coordination

This is a problem common to the administration of agriculture in any context but it becomes still greater in the context of irrigation. In addition to the need for coordination among the various agricultural agencies (with responsibilities for policies in the fields of extension, credit, input supplies, marketing, etc.), there is a further need for coordination between these agencies—especially agricultural extension—and the engineers who have prime responsibility for operating and maintaining the irrigation system. Unfortunately, it is all too common to find agricultural and engineering wings on irrigation projects operating virtually independently of each other. Apart from the more obvious reasons for this (affiliation to different departments and different disciplines), the difficulties are aggravated by the fact that Irrigation is commonly a more powerful, prestigious department than Agriculture, partly because of the high level of capital investment which goes into supporting its design and construction work: this is usually reflected in higher salary scales and a tendency for Irrigation personnel to dominate decisions about important management issues, especially water allocation. There is also the problem that the boundaries of the commanded area, which are the natural ones for Irrigation to operate within, rarely accord closely with those of the civil administrative units on which Agriculture is customarily based. The most favoured way of trying to get round these problems is to establish unified authorities in which a single management agency is responsible for coordinating all development activities within a given command area. But even then, weaknesses tend to persist, especially in the area of water allocation (matching supply and demand) where close collaboration between engineers and agriculturalists is most needed.

(e) Need to impose discipline

Where water is scarce and has to be allocated among a large number of competing private users, most of them small farmers, a good operating agency is called upon to ration it; and this will inevitably lead to a conflict between the objectives of the operating agency and those of the individual water users. We may assume that the agency's objectives will be to maximize overall economic returns to water within the whole project area, while at the same time achieving a high degree of equity in its distribution. This can only be done by supplying each farmer with less water than he wants to meet his own objectives: not only will he want enough water to obtain the highest possible financial returns for himself by operating further up the production function curve (Levine, 1977), but he will usually want still more than that, if possible, as an insurance against risk, for his own private convenience (e.g. in rice areas to reduce labour requirements for weeding) or for some other reason. It follows that even in the best managed irrigation projects, operating staff are likely to be subjected to strong pressures from farmers to supply them with more water than they are entitled to; and these farmers may often have powerful local political backing. If the operating agency is to meet its objectives, staff must therefore be able and willing to impose discipline on competing pressure groups by applying rules impartially and penalizing those who break them. In fact, staff often give way to the pressures placed on them, in the absence of strong commitment at high levels to meet the agency's (stated) objectives, and the result in the worst cases can be a degeneration into "water anarchy", in which disproportionately large amounts of water go to farmers who are more influential and/or favourably located near the head of the system. The staff's difficulties are compounded when controlled operation of the water delivery system is hampered by design deficiencies.

These are broad generalizations. And although specific examples can (and will) be used to illustrate and amplify them, it is obvious that they do not all apply with equal force in all circumstances. Indeed, large irrigation projects in different parts of the developing world exhibit a wide variety of characteristics as a result of the interplay of numerous local factors (physical, technical, economic, social, political). These characteristics in turn affect the kind of management problems most likely to arise in each case and the measures most appropriate for remedying them. But although there are many different management approaches which are available for use in each individual case (in terms of organizational structure, techniques of management control, concentration or diffusion of decision-making responsibilities, etc.) the approaches actually chosen are often poorly adapted to the particular needs of the local situation.

In seeking appropriate solutions in particular cases, the following appear to be among the most important factors to be taken into account:

(i)   technical characteristics of water source (e.g. storage/run-of-river);

(ii)   technical characteristics of delivery system (e.g. high technology/low technology; night storage/24-hour flow);

(iii) physical characteristics (climate; soils; topography);

(iv) drainage requirements;

(v)   intensiveness/extensiveness of cropping patterns for which system has been designed;

(vi) characteristics of watercourse/tertiary command (e.g. regular or irregular farm boundaries; extent of physical control structures; regularity/irregularity of micro-topography);

(vii) water availability in relation to level of demand;

(viii) degree of management control over farmers' choice of cropping patterns;

(ix) level and method of water charges;

(x)   local socio-political factors (social cohesion of farmers at village/channel level; access of farmers to higher-level political support; skewness of farm size/incomes; proportion of owner- and tenant-operated farms);

(xi) level of farmers' agricultural and water management skills.

An illustration of the very different "mix" of management skills which may be required on projects with different characteristics is given in Appendix A, with reference to the eleven factors listed above. Many of these are of course "compound" factors. Further sub-division is required for the purposes of detailed analysis. Particular attention has been given here to the central functions of water allocation and maintenance.

In the short space of this paper it is impossible to do more than indicate the diversity of conditions likely to be encountered in the field. But it may be helpful to consider a few strongly contrasting examples. No attempt will be made to deal with any case in great detail. The main aim is to point up the most significant differences in project characteristics which have a bearing on their management requirements; to illustrate the extent to which project performance can be affected by appropriate or inappropriate management inputs; and also to draw attention to the frequency with which the capacity of project managers to operate effectively is impaired by external factors largely outside their control (e.g. deficiencies in project planning and system design; inadequacy of finance for operation and maintenance; government pricing policies, including low water charges; inadequate legal framework; regulations affecting the salary structures, promotion policies and incentives of staff.

For purposes of simplification, some rather crude categorization or "typologizing" will be used. Though many other bases for categorization could be used (as a glance at the eleven factors will show), some of the more important differences in management requirements can be brought out by reference to the length of time over which a project has been operating. Accordingly, projects will be considered under two main headings: those which have been only recently constructed and those which are relatively long-established. The first category is further sub-divided into projects involving new settlement and those introduced into already settled areas.

RECENTLY CONSTRUCTED PROJECTS

In the initial years of a large irrigation project, farmers' demand for water is likely to be substantially lower than the peak level for which the water delivery system has been designed. So, providing the system has been reasonably well designed and constructed, relatively little administrative effort needs to be devoted to the functions of water allocation and water rationing which become so important at a later stage when demand has built up. A frequent problem is to persuade farmers previously unaccustomed to irrigation (or, in some cases, to agriculture of any kind) to take up the water supplied to them and make productive use of it. In that case, the first priority will be to stimulate demand; and this implies the provision of an effective agricultural extension service (with recourse to specialist advice on water management matters) from the moment the project comes on-stream. As has already been indicated, the indivisability of the project will usually mean mobilizing a large number of staff for this work within a short space of time, and this will often entail substantial staff training programmes beforehand. Meanwhile, the main preoccupation of senior engineering staff is likely to be with sorting out the inevitable technical "teething problems" which are encountered at the start of any large irrigation project. But, even if water allocation presents no immediate difficulties, their subordinates should already be acquainting farmers with the rules and regulations which they will be expected to abide by in the future—a process likely to be assisted by the formation of local water users' groups. Failure to inculcate respect for a disciplined approach to water distribution from the outset is likely to be a recipe for disaster later on. During this period, the engineers and agriculturalists should also be giving joint thought to the planning of increasingly sophisticated techniques of water distribution as the project progresses, while at the same time designing improved structures and micro-layouts at the tertiary level of the system to enable these new techniques to be effectively applied. Both technically and economically it makes sense to delay the refinements of watercourse/tertiary development until after a project comes on-stream (e.g. initially there is no need for sophisticated control structures at the watercourse outlet: simple pipes may be enough). This gradualist approach is one which has been deliberately adopted, with apparent success, on the Muda project in Malaysia (which, after more than 10 years of operation, still supplies farmers with water on a field-to-field basis from lateral canals 1 ¼ miles apart). But it should not be confused with the approach which neglects adequate development at the watercourse level entirely.

On new projects which suffer from major deficiencies in design and construction there may often be little that the management staff (either on the agricultural and irrigation side) can do to mitigate the inevitable problems that arise. In such cases, it is important that the true causes of poor performance should be diagnosed early and the appropriate action be taken as soon as possible. Otherwise much time and effort may be wasted on looking for "management" solutions where none exist.

Settlement schemes

If they are to have any chance of success, agricultural development schemes in newly-settled areas—whether they are irrigated or not— call for detailed and comprehensive planning, in the social and economic spheres as well as the physical and technical ones. One finds as a result that, although many such schemes have met with difficulty or failure, those which have done well have usually benefited from a lot of careful thought about effective management systems and procedures. A common characteristic of these schemes is a high degree of official management control over all agricultural and irrigation operations: a single agency provides the farmers with all the inputs required (including water) and recovers its costs by deducting them from the value of their marketed output. This kind of "closed" system is only operable where a large proportion of farmers' output consists of high-value cash crops which can only be sold through a single marketing channel controlled by the management agency. Cropping patterns, crop rotations, the timing of agricultural operations, etc., are all decided by the agency; the farmers' responsibilities are often confined to the execution of certain labour-intensive crop husbandry activities. On many schemes in anglophone Africa, the enforcement of strict discipline is greatly assisted by the insecurity of the farmers' land tenure: they are usually tenants licensed by the scheme management, on an annually renewable basis, and can be threatened with eviction if judged to have performed poorly.

The Mwea Scheme in Kenya is one on which an extreme form of this highly controlled "integrated management" approach has been employed. Its performance has shown that such an approach can be very effective, both in terms of stimulating high levels of production and raising farmers' incomes, in the initial years of settlement when the farmers have had little or no previous experience of irrigated agriculture—though in Mwea it also involved the imposition of serious social stresses on the farm family (Chambers and Morris, 1973). On the other hand, a common failing of this approach appears to be that, once its basic rules and procedures have been established, there is a tendency for its institutions to become ossified. There has been evidence of this on the Gezira scheme in the Sudan, which was established in the mid-1920s but underwent no major changes in its institutions or cropping patterns until very recently: it is only in the last 4 or 5 years that significant steps have been taken to diversify and intensify the traditional cotton-dominated cropping pattern and to make corresponding changes in management structures and practices which would allow tenants more autonomy.

Two of the factors likely to contribute most to institutional stagnation over time are the short-term tenancy agreements and the dominance of a single cash crop—factors which both tend to have an important influence on the effectiveness of management in the initial stages of a settlement scheme. Of these, the tenancy factor appears to be the most damaging in the long run, since it reduces farmers' incentives to invest or innovate. A preferable approach would be one in which settlers could purchase land in instalments over time. This would allow the management agency gradually to devolve some of its responsibilities to farmers as their experience increases and free some of its staff for more productive employment elsewhere. Irrigation settlement schemes with provision for land purchase are often found in post-land reform contexts (e.g. Lower Medjerda, Tunisia; San Lorenzo, Peru).

This suggests an important general lesson which can be learnt from the experience of the more successful irrigated settlement schemes—one which applies equally to irrigation schemes of other kinds where a similar concentration of management control would be inconceivable. It is very simple: in the early stages of any large irrigation project strong official direction—both technical and administrative—is an essential ingredient of success, but with the passage of time (with increases in farmer knowledge and income, better and more varied market opportunities) increasing benefits are likely to come from decentralization of decision-making and more farmer participation.

Support for this view (from a very different context) can be found by examining the way in which the highly successful system of irrigation management now used in Taiwan has developed over the past 50 years. Despite the government's decision in 1975 to take control of the management of the country's Irrigation Associations from the farmers' representatives who were previously in charge (apparently a temporary measure), the members of the Associations still have many responsibilities devolved to them, especially at the "Small Group" (150 ha) level; and there continues to be a great deal of discussion about administrative issues and technical issues between Small Group leaders and the official management. However, the sophisticated institutional arrangements which are currently found in Taiwan are a relatively recent (post World War II) phenomenon. They have evolved over a long period as part of a complex process of political, economic and social change. During the period of Japanese rule (1895-1945), when Taiwan was developed into a major rice exporter to Japan, the management of irrigation was highly authoritarian. To stimulate agricultural production, the government relied on close technical supervision of farmers and the police were called upon, if necessary, to enforce new cultivation practices or cropping patterns. Though they were established in 1922, it was not until the end of Japanese rule that the Irrigation Associations became self-governing; and the present widespread practice of rotational irrigation (which is associated with the use of increasingly sophisticated technology) was introduced only in the mid-1950s.

It may seem a fairly elementary point that the management of irrigation projects should be considered as an evolutionary process, with a progression over time from a relatively high degree of central control towards increasing farmer participation and autonomy of decision-making. But failure to observe this pattern is extremely common, especially where irrigation has been introduced into already settled areas.

Schemes in areas of existing settlement

Whereas the planners of irrigated settlement schemes are able to start off with what is virtually a *tabula rasa*, those who are entrusted with the task of introducing irrigation into already settled areas (the norm in most of Asia) are obliged to contend with a much more complex set of social issues. Systems of private land tenure are already in existence; farm boundaries have been established, usually on a very irregular pattern; and farmers are accustomed to making their own decisions about what to grow and when. This presents problems to the more technical aspects of planning and design. E.g. does one attempt to carry out land consolidation and land shaping before the introduction of irrigation in order to establish "rationalized" rectangular farm layouts from the start—a process often involving protracted legal negotiations as well as substantial capital expenditure; or does one start off by accepting a technically "second-best" solution, with the aim of working towards gradual improvement and intensification of watercourse infrastructure as the growing demand for water increases the need for reductions in water losses? Furthermore, introduction of irrigation into settled areas makes it impossible for the prospective managers of these projects to apply many of the cruder mechanisms for control which are commonly used on settlement schemes. Yet in the initial years of these projects certain basic rules and disciplines have to be imposed and effective methods must be devised for the purpose. Although the farmers in the project area will have had previous agricultural experience, they will be familiar neither with the technical refinements of irrigated agriculture (crop water requirements; techniques of water application) nor with the disciplines associated with water distribution and water sharing. Even the fact that local social groupings are already extant (village organizations, cooperatives, etc.) may not necessarily be of any great advantage, since the most effective local irrigation institutions tend to be channel-based rather than village-based. But where social cohesion is already good, water users' groups should be relatively easy to introduce. Intensive farmer training programmes are therefore required (and this implies large inputs of well-trained staff)—especially so if the intended system of irrigation management is one which demands adherence to a preordained cropping pattern or to regulations restricting the cultivation of certain crops to designated zones. The effectiveness of these administrative measures can be greatly enhanced by other factors too—especially favourable economic policies (which would allow, among other things, for the imposition of high water charges. And their success is of course dependent on the fundamental prerequisites of an adequate technical base.

In these circumstances, it might be expected that particular attention would be paid at the planning stage to studying in detail the particular social conditions of the locality to be developed and identifying the organizational structures and management procedures most likely to produce successful results in those conditions. However, the need for such an approach is almost invariably underestimated. In many cases, future management considerations are virtually ignored: Chambers (1975) cites a multi-volume planning report for a major irrigation project in Sri Lanka which contains a mere 1½ pages on organization and management. In other cases rather more thought may be given to management, but the recommendations made on the subject are often perfunctory and stereotyped—being closely modelled either on past precedent within the country concerned or on current international fashions. In either event, the planning and design process tends to be dominated by technical experts (especially engineers), with economists being called in to calculate the costs and benefits of what is technically (but not necessarily socially or administratively) feasible. In their justification of a project, planners will assume certain future cropping patterns; but (with a population of numerous independent farm operators) what administrative mechanisms will be used to induce widespread adoption of these cropping patterns? What procedures will be used for allocating water? What specialized staff training programmes will be required to apply these procedures and provide farmers with advice on field-level water management? Few planning reports supply more than vague or routine answers to these questions.

The consequences of this kind of planning, which takes little account of local social conditions or needs, are inevitably depressing. No doubt a veil has been drawn over many of the worst instances, but at least two of the case studies presented at a recent ODI workshop on irrigation management reported familiar symptoms: insufficient finance and staffing for operation and maintenance; minimal training of irrigation staff in operational procedures; grossly inadequate provision of agricultural extension staff; slow up-take of

water by farmers leading to much wastage; a high incidence of water disputes (Zabala (1976)
on the Chimborazo irrigation district, Ecuador, where the overall water use efficiency
was reported as 27%; and Ali (1976) on the Ganges-Kobadak project in Bangladesh).

In such circumstances, the larger the project, the greater the problems: Chambers (1975)
has been strongly critical of recent large-scale irrigation development in Sri Lanka, as has
Motooka, of large river basin projects in Thailand. But the most sustained and scathing
attacks on the engineering-dominated approach to planning have been made by Vohra (1975)
in India, with particular reference to the spate of large new irrigation projects designed
and constructed in the 1950s and 1960s. His criticisms have been directed not only at
their size ("the disease of giganticism") but at their essential incompleteness: the engineers'
view was that their job was only to design and construct the main and secondary canal
systems; drainage was supposed to be the responsibility of the agricultural department
and minor canalization and land shaping was left to the farmers to carry out themselves.
The results, as I have had occasion to observe in the Chambal areas of Rajasthan and
Madhya Pradesh, were projects which, because of their fundamental technical deficiencies,
became virtually unmanageable. Drainage was never installed; in the heavy clay soil
conditions of Chambal this led to rapid waterlogging. And layouts at watercourse level
were inadequate to ensure reliable water deliveries to many of the farmers, owing to the
unevenness of the micro-topography. To overcome these difficulties, farmers in the head-
reaches were permitted to install additional "illegal" outlets, with the result that tail-enders
usually went short, water anarchy arose and any possibility of allocating water on a rational
or equitable basis was removed. Now, under India's new Command Area Development
programme (which is designed to remedy the major faults identified by Vohra in the country's
approach to the planning and execution of irrigation projects), strenuous attempts are
being made to rehabilitate these projects, both physically and institutionally. There are,
of course, large new projects which are honourable exceptions to the rule and are exempt
from most of the strictures contained in the preceding paragraphs. For example, both on
the Muda project in Malaysia and the Upper Pampanga project in the Philippines considerable thought has been given to developing detailed management procedures and
training programmes (though not until some time after the planning and construction
phases were completed).

A very different kind of fault which can ensue from an excessively technocratic approach
to irrigation planning is that of "over-design". Here, the technology introduced at the
beginning of a project is simply too sophisticated (and costly) for the relatively modest
requirements of farmers during its initial stages. Moreover, it may well be beyond the
technical and administrative capacities of the local staff to operate and maintain it properly.
Such development generally represents an inappropriate transfer of modern technology,
though in fairness to many of the international consultancy firms which are employed to
advise on the design of these systems, the strongest pressure for "ultra-modernity" often
comes from their clients: most of the commissions for high-technology surface delivery
systems come from oil-rich countries of the Middle East, where investment in automation
is commonly seen not only as a virtue in itself but also as a substitute for inexperienced
semi-skilled system operators. But automated systems are also found in parts of francophone
Africa. Where such systems are installed, they generally require initial management by
foreign advisers. In the best cases, these advisers will introduce intensive training programmes
for local staff. But a common criticism of this kind of approach is that, however successful

such a project may turn out to be when judged in terms of its own internal performance, the level of its technical and managerial expertise will be so much higher than that of the rest of the agricultural sector surrounding it that it will become an "oasis" scheme, with no external demonstration effect and limited replicability; moreover, its success may depend on depriving the rest of the country's agriculture of its best management staff. Elsewhere, the imbalance between high technology and low levels of farmer sophistication can often lead to disappointing results: Levine reports that on the Dez pilot irrigation project in Iran ("a comprehensive system, with a full range of controls, measuring structures, organizational structure, and all the other accoutrements of a large modern system"), average water use efficiency, after 6 years of operation, was between 11% and 15% (Levine, 1977).

LONG-ESTABLISHED SYSTEMS

Many of the major irrigation systems in the developing world have been in existence for a long time, especially in parts of Asia. For example, the basic network of the extensive canal systems in North West India and Pakistan was established about a century ago; and many others were developed during the first four decades of this century. Most of them have undergone subsequent modifications from time to time. But, as a result of the length of time during which they have been in operation, there tends to be a certain similarity about the kind of management issues with which they are typically confronted: farmers are generally attuned to the rhythms of irrigated agriculture (though their techniques may not necessarily be particularly sophisticated); certain formal or informal rules about aspects of watercourse management have been established by irrigation staff or the farmers themselves; demand for water has reached a level which calls for careful planning and scheduling of supplies if it is to be met; and water allocation has therefore become— or ought to have become—the major preoccupation of project management. It is therefore usual to find certain established and well-defined procedures for water allocation prescribed for use on these older projects.

The techniques according to which water is allocated (or is supposed to be allocated) vary greatly from place to place. This can be illustrated by reference to three cases with which I have become familiar through recent research work:

(a) In the low-rainfall, mainly wheat/cotton region of North West India and Pakistan no official restrictions are placed on farmers' choices of cropping pattern. But because the canal systems are very extended and their design intensities extremely low, the water delivered to farmers is severely rationed, in accordance with a pattern of rotation at the watercourse level (called *"warabandi"*): this entitles each farmer to water only within a certain designated period each week (provided water happens to be flowing into his watercourse at the time), the entitlement being proportional to the area of land he operates. As a result, his cropping choices are effectively limited by the rigid scheduling and small amounts of water he receives (Reidinger, 1974). If operated according to plan, this system of water allocation has the virtue that it is equitable; it is easy to operate (detailed knowledge about farmers' cropping patterns are reckoned unnecessary for the purposes of water distribution since they are assumed to be uniform); and discipline is easy to enforce (the *warabandi* schedules are supposed to be established by irrigation officials). On the other hand, the fact that farmers' actual demands have so little influence over allocation patterns implies a minimal need for interaction between irrigation staff on the one hand and agricultural staff and farmers on the other: whatever limited possibilities there may be for increasing the flexibility of water distribution are likely to remain unexplored.

(b) In Java, an area of relatively high rainfall where irrigation is used as a supplementary source of water—principally for rice but also for other crops with substantially lower water requirements—a complicated system of water allocation is in use which is intended to provide a means of responding to the actual cropping patterns farmers have chosen to adopt. Since there is usually insufficient water in the "dry" season for all farmers to grow rice (the preferred crop), restrictions are placed on the areas permitted to plant rice— these may be rotated from year to year; but otherwise free choice of cropping is allowed. Every 10 days, farmers' representatives report to local irrigation officials their estimates of the actual area under different crops within each watercourse command and that area's water requirements are then calculated on the basis of certain water duties associated with each crop. Whatever water supplies are available within a given 10-day period are then supposed to be divided between watercourses in proportion to the pattern of estimated demand (Taylor and Pasandaran, 1976). Such a system requires a great deal of detailed calculation and measurement by junior irrigation officials and, if it is to work as intended, calls for a high degree of supervision and control from more senior staff. In theory, the system should allow great flexibility and minimize water losses. But if supervision is lacking, and if restrictions on rice cultivation are not rigorously enforced, the junior officials are likely to come under heavy pressure from competing farmer groups to provide extra water and the results may be very inequitable.

(c) Taiwan's physical and social conditions are in many ways similar to Java's, but its methods of water allocation are very different. There, in areas of water shortage, only a certain proportion of all watercourses are entitled to enough water for rice in a given year; the rest are obliged to grow less water-demanding crops. In accordance with a set pattern of crop rotation, each watercourse obtains the same number of entitlements to rice water within a 3-year period. This system has the virtue of being simple to operate, once the initial detailed plans have been established; and farmers have a predictable and well-devised pattern of supply within which to plan their farming operations. Farmers with entitlements to water for rice are not obliged to grow rice; on the other hand, they may not transfer any unused part of their entitlement elsewhere. To the extent that farmers choose not to adhere to the planned cropping pattern, there may therefore be some water wastage which could have been avoided through the use of a more flexible and responsive system.

There are many good reasons why methods of water allocation differ so widely: differences in local physical, technical and social conditions. But a less good reason which may be an important factor in many cases is the nature of past external cultural influences: the method of canal operation in North West India and Pakistan still owes a lot to British legislation embodied in the Northern India Canal and Drainage Act of 1873; the Javanese system was developed under the Dutch; the Taiwan system under the Japanese. This introduces an element of fortuitousness into the way in which allocation methods have been adopted and may in itself be sufficient justification for asking, in each case one meets, the following series of questions:

(a) What are the prescribed procedures? What are their objectives?

(b) Are the prescribed procedures being applied? Are the original objectives being met or have they been replaced by new ones?

(c) Could better results be achieved by using other procedures which are more appropriate to local needs? Would it be feasible to try to introduce them?

The point has already been made in this paper that the management of a system can only be as good as the physical condition of that system allows it to be. A common feature of older systems is that their designs have become incapable of meeting the demands of modern agriculture (e.g. the many North West Indian systems which were designed to spread water over a wide area to prevent famines but cannot provide the much more intensive water supply patterns which HYV wheats require). Or alternatively, many of them have suffered physical deterioration as a result of poor maintenance. In the one case, remodelling is required, in the other rehabilitation. This raises the question on many of the older systems as to how much improvement in performance is possible by essentially management means and how much it depends on technical solutions. In most cases there will be short-comings on both fronts and one's judgement as to which is the more serious may often depend on one's disciplinary affiliations.

In recent years increasing attention has been paid by governments and donor agencies to programmes designed to improve the performance of older systems. The principal remedies favoured have included the following:

(i) *Technical improvements*
   (a) remodelling/rehabilitation of main canal system (additional control structures, etc.);
   (b) improved physical layout at tertiary level ("on-farm development").

(ii) *Organizational changes*
   (a) formation of single coordinating agency at project level;
   (b) strengthened agricultural extension;
   (c) creation of formal "water users" associations.

(iii) *Economic/financial measures:*
   (a) higher water rates;
   (b) larger budget allocations for operation and maintenance.

(iv) *Operational procedures:*
   (a) rotational irrigation at the tertiary level;
   (b) improved techniques of water application at farm level.

This appears to be a very comprehensive list, covering both technical and management improvements: on many projects all or nearly all the elements may be combined, as part of a single "package". But on close observation it will be seen that one form of improvement is conspicuously missing; and that is improvement of operational procedures on the main delivery system—precisely the area of "man management" on which much of this paper has been focused. The omission is extraordinary, because there is abundant evidence that this is an area of great weakness on many large projects and may often be the single area of greatest weakness: Reidinger (1974) has commented on it in North West India, Wade (1976) in Andhra Pradesh, Harriss (1974) and Chambers (1975) in Sri Lanka; and Valera and Wickham (1976) have described a piece of experimental field research in the

Philippines which demonstrated remarkable returns to improvements in management procedures alone. Yet governments and donor agencies prefer to cling to the belief that the main problems associated with the main system are technical ones and can be solved by technical means; the main management problems, they appear to believe, are to be found at the watercourse and farm levels. There is no good evidence for this. It is true, that, where detailed measurements have been made of water losses at different stages of the delivery system, they have generally been shown to be considerably greater at the watercourse and farm levels than in the main conveyance system (see e.g. Bos and Nugteren, 1974). However, it is not legitimate to assume from this (as many people appear to) that the *causes* of these higher losses at the end of the system are to be found exclusively in bad watercourse and on-farm management; many of them may be the consequences of deficient management of the main distribution system (untimeliness, unpredictability of water deliveries, etc.). It may therefore be possible for a system to be described as having a high "conveyance efficiency" in a conventional engineering sense (because losses in the main distribution system are low) and yet for it to be operated very inefficiently. Clearly the use of "efficiency" in this specialized sense can be extremely misleading as a guide to policy-making, since it relates only to the *location* of water losses and takes no account of their causes. The identification of the causes of watercourse and on-farm losses—and hence their remedies—requires far more than purely technical research. No one would wish to deny that both physical and institutional improvements are often required at these lower levels of the system. But on the other hand, the benefits to be obtained from improvements at these levels is bound to be greatly reduced if deficiencies in the operation of the main system are overlooked or ignored. The same applies to other elements in the package: e.g. farmers will be unwilling to pay high water charges unless water deliveries are reliable and predictable.

The explanations for this blind spot are numerous. They probably include a natural bias towards technical solutions: realization that the management of the main system is a sensitive area and that it is safer and easier to shift the emphasis onto tertiary development; the difficulty of analysing and identifying management weaknesses in the short time usually allotted to consultants and advisers; and (though this is rarely admitted) a preference—among donor agencies and governments—for capital rather than recurrent investment.

SMALL COMMUNALLY-OPERATED SYSTEMS

Small "indigenous" surface-water systems which are operated by groups of farmers have been favourite objects of study by anthropologists and sociologists. For a guide to the literature, see Coward (1976). They are widely found in upland river valleys in many parts of the world; those in South-East Asia have attracted particular attention. They are typically self-contained systems of up to 200-300 ha, dependent for their water supplies on simple diversion weirs made of boulders or brushwood, which are designed, constructed, operated and maintained by small farming communities. Because of their upstream location their water supplies tend to be abundant compared with those of larger river basin systems.

In contrast to the larger publicly-operated systems, the communal systems are generally well-organized: man-management is not one of their problems. Indeed, Coward has suggested that there are certain organizational principles embodied in the practices employed on communal systems which could usefully be incorporated into the management of much larger systems. He has pointed in particular to three important features which are common to most systems of this type: (i) They have an "accountable leadership": leaders of each local group are selected by members of that group, their performance is periodically reviewed by them and they are compensated for their services directly by the group. (ii) The systems, although themselves small, are usually sub-divided into smaller sub-units, each with its own leader: "management intensity" is very high. Moreover, each of these "mini-units" corresponds to a discrete physical sub-section of the larger system. (iii) The systems are rarely coterminous with village boundaries: they are channel-based, not village-based. Attempts by outside agencies to organize local irrigation groups on a village basis may therefore often run into difficulties (Coward, 1976).

On the other hand, there is nearly always considerable scope for improving the technical characteristics of communal systems: and there is a growing need for such improvement in areas where population pressure is causing increasing demands to be made on common sources of river water. For example, on the Balinese *subaks*, which are probably the most sophisticated and complex of communal systems (Geertz, 1967; Birkelbach, 1973), the Indonesian Public Works Department has designed and constructed permanent diversion structures to replace several of the temporary weirs previously constructed and maintained by the *subak* members; more are planned. Investigations are also being made into the possibilities of reducing water losses through the installation of control structures and measuring devices within the *subak* areas. The benefits which the farmers can obtain from the permanent weirs appear to be clear, for substantial time which was previously lost at the end of each rainy season on repairing and reconstructing the temporary weirs can now be used for earlier and more timely rice cultivation. But other changes which may appear desirable on technical grounds (e.g. combining the offtakes of two *subaks*) could well create social and organizational problems unless the plans to implement them are carefully discussed with the farmers beforehand. Interventions of this kind obviously require delicacy and tact on the part of government, since it is in everyone's interest that the internal affairs of the *subak* (especially water allocation, which is calculated in great detail and with particular concern for equity) should remain in the hands of its members and that the intricate management systems which they have built up should be allowed to continue and develop. Unfortunately, it has been a common experience elsewhere that governments' attempts to incorporate communal systems into larger projects tend to lead to the disintegration of previously dynamic water users' groups, because they lost most of their original responsibilities in the process and are given no new ones to take their place.

Many of the points made above with reference to communal systems based on hill stream diversions also apply to those which depend for their water supplies on local storage "tanks". Chambers (1974) has described the attention to detail and equity in water distribution which is to be found on some village-operated tank irrigation schemes in South India and Sri Lanka, though others have encountered technical difficulties which, in the absence of government support, they have been unable to overcome on their own.

SYSTEMS DEPENDENT ON GROUNDWATER

The two most obvious advantages which groundwater systems have over surface-water systems have already been mentioned: greater divisibility of investment and greater operational flexibility. Both of these have important implications for management. However, the use of groundwater becomes an option only under certain aquifer conditions; and it is usually a more expensive source of water than surface supplies. There are three main issues in groundwater development and management: (i) alternative well and pump technologies; (ii) public *versus* private ownership and operation of wells; and (iii) aquifer management. All are interconnected.

In theory, where there is a choice between using public or private tubewells to exploit the same relatively deep freshwater aquifer (e.g. as in parts of Pakistan and Indian Punjab), the larger wells which can be installed by the public sector ought to be more efficient (in economic terms) than the smaller wells likely to be favoured by private investors, owing to their longer life and lower per unit pumping costs. Whereas the public wells are fitted with multi-stage pumps, the size of private wells is usually limited by the use of centrifugal pumps. The difference in discharge capacity may be of the order of 3 : 0.5 cusec. Unless social conditions favour cooperative investment by a group of farmers (uncommon in Pakistan or North West India), private investors will prefer the smaller pumps because of their lower cost and the closer correlation between their supplies and the demands of a single farm; maintenance and repair facilities will also be much more easily available. Evidence suggests that, in practice, the performance of public wells tends to fall well below planners' expectations, largely owing to "poor management". What this usually means, in effect, is that they are often badly maintained and are nearly always operated rather inflexibly, with much less sensitivity to changes in the pattern of demand for water than private wells (see, e.g. Mellor and Moorti, 1971): in contrast to the public tubewell operator, private well-owners have to bear the full costs involved and therefore reduce wastage to a minimum by pumping only when their crops require water. In the worst cases, if he is not properly supervised, a public tubewell operator may even go so far as to obstruct farmers from getting water when they require it by abusing his position of local monopoly and stimulating "breakdowns" which he will refuse to "put right" until recompensed.

It does not necessarily follow from this that, in the aquifer conditions described, groundwater exploitation ought always to be left to the private sector. So far we have only given thought to efficiency of water use. When it comes to equity of water distribution, it can be argued that—especially where groundwater supplies are capable of being used in conjunction with surface-water—a single fully planned and integrated system of operation under public control is likely to produce a more even spread of benefits than one in which wells are operated privately and independently of the (public) surface system. Once again, this argument *ought* to be true—provided those who are responsible for managing the public system behave as the planners would like them to. In Taiwan, where management staff are notably responsive to farmers' needs, it almost certainly is true. There, Irrigation Associations with suitable groundwater conditions have installed deep wells which are pumped directly into the surface delivery system and are operated in close conjunction with the pattern of surface supplies. (Strictly speaking, Irrigation Associations are not government organizations and are therefore not "public" bodies in that sense. However, in this context their functions and responsibilities are clearly analagous.) Most of these wells are concentrated toward the tails of lateral or sub-lateral canals, so that tail-end farmers likely to be vulnerable to deficiencies in surface-water supplies can have access to supplementary groundwater when required. In many other societies, however, a similar concern for equity may be harder to find among management staff and it is not impossible that in some cases smaller farmers might be better off under a system where they have to buy water on a private basis from larger farmers—however imperfect such a system may be.

Under a different set of freshwater aquifer conditions, where the water table is high and easily exploitable by shallow wells (e.g. as in parts of the eastern Gangetic plain and in Bangladesh), the case in favour of promoting development on a private basis may be rather more clear-cut. With reference to Bangladesh, Biggs *et al.* (1977) have been critical of the emphasis which the government, with the backing of external donor agencies, has been giving to the promotion of publicly-operated deep tubewells of the type being employed in Pakistan. They argue that this is a case of inappropriate technology transfer, not only because the present high water table in Bangladesh renders deep tubewells costly and unnecessary but also because local land holdings are extremely fragmented: it is therefore much easier to organize efficient water distribution from a large number of small sources than from much fewer (relatively inflexible) big ones. The authors point out that private farmers in Bangladesh are already making widespread use of highly divisible low-cost irrigation technologies (shallow wells, low-lift surface pumps, etc.), yet no research has been done on them and official plans for irrigation development take no account of them (cf. the bamboo tubewell developed and disseminated in Bihar, with no government assistance: Clay, 1972; Dommen, 1975). They suggest that the government's immediate priority should be to concentrate on the improvement and development of these existing technologies and to make them widely available: despite their relatively low cost, this would entail making special credit provisions for the smallest farmers to ensure that they could obtain access to them. Then, at a later date, when increased pumping has led to a lowering of the aquifer, thought could begin to be given to introducing larger and deeper wells.

By contrast, there are certain other aquifer conditions under which there is an incontrovertible case for well operation by a public agency: for example, when the quality of the groundwater is too poor to be used for irrigation unless it has first been carefully mixed with surface supplies; or when (whatever its quality) it has risen so close to the surface that it has to be pumped out and kept below a certain level for drainage reasons.

This leads on to the issue of aquifer management in general. There can be no doubt that groundwater surveys, the monitoring of groundwater extractions and the establishment of regulations and controls concerning exploitation of the aquifer should all be government responsibilities. To meet its responsibilities with regard to aquifer management a government can adopt one of two approaches: it can exercise direct control over groundwater extractions by acting as the principal or exclusive operating agency (an approach which entails high administrative costs, especially where groundwater reserves are extensive, and often leads, at best, to the provision of a somewhat inflexible service to farmers); or it can encourage private well development but set limits to its expansion through strict legislation and the use of pricing policies which reflect the true increases in pumping costs as the aquifer level declines.

Certain groundwater conditions have already been mentioned for which direct public control of the aquifer is mandatory. It is also a necessary condition for the success of any comprehensive programme designed to achieve optimal conjunctive use of surface and groundwater sources (Stoner, 1976). Careful manipulation of the aquifer (involving the maintenance of a close balance between pumping and recharge) is a central feature of such a programme. It may be worth adding that the programme's success will also depend on certain stringent administrative conditions being met: not only on sufficient technical expertise at higher management levels to prepare the basic water scheduling plans but also on sufficient dedication on the part of field staff to implement them efficiently and fairly. Another elementary condition is that the same public agency should be responsible for the planning and operation of the two different water sources—yet this is often not the case.

The most obvious benefits likely to be obtainable from private groundwater development are flexibility of operation and hence relatively high efficiencies of water use. But the value of this can become very questionable if the government fails to establish firm rules and limitations within which private groundwater users are obliged to operate. These can be applied through prohibiting private well development except under government licence: restrictions can be placed not only on well locations but also on pump capacities. The latter restriction has important implications for equity of access to groundwater as well as being an effective means of controlling aquifer levels. Without such controls (and special programmes to help smaller farmers obtain pumping equipment), private groundwater development becomes a "free for all", with larger farmers taking the lead in exploiting the limited water resources and then maintaining their advantage as the aquifer becomes progressively overpumped by moving on to increasingly sophisticated technologies which their poorer neighbours cannot afford. The dangers of failing to provide effective public controls over private groundwater extraction are vividly illustrated by the case of the Wadi Dhuleil project in Jordan, where a particularly rapid decline in water levels occurred owing to the restricted nature of the aquifer (Carruthers *et al.*, 1974). Other examples abound.

Legislative measures to prevent overpumping can be usefully reinforced by appropriate pricing policies. In theory it should be possible to limit groundwater extractions by pricing techniques alone, without having recourse to other forms of control. But, despite farmers' demonstrated willingness to pay high prices for the privilege of pumping their own water, governments—under pressure from larger farmers—are generally reluctant to promote private well development without concealed subsidies; and even if such a policy were faithfully applied, it would still fail to deal with the problem of unequal access to groundwater by smaller farmers.

Many governments' unwillingness to act against the interests of their large farmer constituencies also explains why they are so frequently half-hearted in applying legislative controls. This serves to emphasize once again that good groundwater management, like good surface-water management, is impossible unless there is a commitment at the highest political levels to serve the interests of all water users and not only minority pressure groups. And the point applies with equal force whether the day-to-day groundwater operations are in private or public hands.

RESEARCH AND TRAINING PRIORITIES

Just as good irrigation management calls for the closest collaboration among the different parties involved (irrigation officials, agricultural officials, farmers), each of whom has his own perspective and area of specialist knowledge, so research on irrigation management must be genuinely and fully interdisciplinary. It must also be carried out in such a way that it has an impact on policy and leads to effective action. It has been the contention of this paper that irrigation management has been a neglected area of study and that its "man-management" aspects in particular have been ignored, underestimated or consciously avoided at critical stages in the decision-making process—both when new projects are being planned and when existing projects are being improved. This is partly because there is a natural tendency for the views of the technical expert to dominate where matters of irrigation development policy are concerned; and partly because investigations into "man-management" tend to be both time-consuming and politically delicate. There is therefore a large and important gap to be filled by social scientists with a special interest in analysing and seeking to improve the performance and management of irrigation schemes.

But while it may be easy enough (perhaps even fashionable) to say that irrigation management is too serious a subject to be left to the engineers, it is equally necessary to stress that it is far too important—and complex—to be dealt with by social scientists on their own. The need is for people who will work closely with the technical experts, not ones who will merely snipe at them from the sidelines. Unless the people chosen to do the work are of an exceptional calibre, I would accord low priority at present to "academic" case-study research on irrigation matters by independent social scientists, for the following reasons:

(a) Most social scientists on their own lack the necessary specialist knowledge to understand the finer technical aspects of the subject.

(b) The kind of "findings" they are likely to come up with may be exciting to them but will tend to be banal and predictable to most people with extensive practical experience of irrigation management: we are no longer in need of further "discoveries" that farmers in the head-reaches get more water than those at the tail; that farmers are prone to stealing water and offering bribes to officials; that larger farmers have better access to, and exploit the benefits of, new technology before smaller farmers—these should be points of departure for research, not its conclusions.

(c) A detailed understanding of the workings of the "irrigation bureaucracy" requires access to official documents and extensive interviews with staff; this is much easier to achieve if one is a member of a consultative team which has been accorded permission by government to carry out such investigations than if one is an independent outside researcher.

(d) Most research of this kind is likely to have little influence on the more hard-headed policy-makers, either because it will be easy to dismiss on the grounds of being insufficiently well-informed on technical matters ((a) above) or of contributing little new to the sum of human knowledge ((b) above); or, more probably, because they will never see it in the first place.

What, then, appear to be the most effective ways in which interdisciplinary research programmes could be developed and used to influence government policies in the field of irrigation management? I see two main possiblities: (a) the establishment of Regional Research and Training Centres, whose main object would be to investigate the merits of different irrigation technologies (both surface- and groundwater) under different physical, economic and social conditions, with particular reference to their implications for management; and (b) the introduction of social scientists with special responsibilities for studying management issues into irrigation consultancy teams, with the object of developing "action research" and management training programmes.

Of these two propositions, the first is obviously the more ambitious. However, there appears to be a very urgent need for research (which would most logically be done on an agro-climatic regional basis) on certain fundamental aspects of irrigation design, onto which further research on management could be grafted. For example, in the predominantly rice-growing areas of monsoon Asia there seem to be wide variations in the design criteria used by the many different consultants who are engaged to advise governments on new irrigation development. One of the objects of a Regional Centre would be to carry out field research on the basis of which consistent design criteria could be established for use within the region. But in addition to carrying out such basic technical research, the Centres would provide excellent opportunities for interdisciplinary research, on a comparative basis, into the consequences for management of different technologies and design decisions. The results of the research, both on the technical and management side, would be used to develop training programmes for irrigation planners and management personnel within the region.

The idea behind the second proposition is that, in cases where governments show interest in receiving advice about the management aspects of their irrigation projects, they should be provided with a fully interdisciplinary team including a social scientist with specific responsibility for studying "man-management" issues. Provided the initial identification study produced proposals which the government was interested in following up, two further stages of the work would follow: a period of "action research", involving experiments with alternative management procedures in the field; and finally the establishment of a national training programme. In most cases, the whole process could be expected to take at least 2 or 3 years.

The object of the first-stage study would be to identify the extent to which the performance of irrigation projects in the country concerned might be improved through better management methods, either with or without related improvements to the technical infrastructure. This would mean starting with an evaluation of the present performance of a selected project or projects, with special emphasis on the performance of the water delivery system. If it was judged to fall substantially short of what it was physically capable of, the reasons for its shortcomings would need to be identified: these might well include factors beyond the control of project management as well as deficiencies in management procedures. On the other hand, the project might be judged incapable of good operation owing to faults in design or other technical factors. In either event, comprehensive proposals would then be put forward for action designed to produce conditions conducive to good management in the future.

At present there is no recognized common methodology for evaluating the management aspects of irrigation projects, but it is the object of a World Bank financed research study which I am currently engaged on, to try to develop one. (World Bank Research Project No. 671/34: Comparative study of the management and organisation of irrigation projects.) For some people the notion of trying to evaluate something as intangible as "management" appears to present major problems. According to Moris (1976), economic planners are particularly apt to be puzzled by what "management" consists of:

Cost-benefit models . . . do not deal intrinsically with *the managerial process* at all, but rather with the surface measurement of the products of such activity . . . . It is a common failing of economists to confuse management with its results, so that again and again the focus is upon the substance of rational decision making and not the process that led to and effected these optimal choices. The real essence of effective management never becomes explicit; "management" remains a mysterious residual factor to trot out at the end as one of the preconditions for effective implementation of rational planning.

But, while it is true that conceptual difficulties arise when one is considering irrigation management in general and rather abstract terms, particularly with regard to the establishment of "standards of good management", there are no excessively complicated problems of method attached to the collection and interpretation of information once one reaches the field and becomes immersed in particular cases. The task of trying to identify the objectives, functions and responsibilities of different members in a management hierarchy calls mainly for patience, tact, a feel for the locality, and time—more time than conventional consultancy studies usually allow. And it is important to remember that the purpose of asking people questions about their work is not only to collect "hard data"—the customary object of many researchers—but also to assess their attitudes and their understanding of what it is they are supposed to be doing.

On the assumption that possibilities for improvement in management have been identified, much more detailed study could be carried out during the second-stage action research period. What is envisaged here is work of the kind done by Wickham and his colleagues in the Philippines: a research team would work closely with irrigation and agricultural staff on a selected project for an extended period, with the object of introducing and testing new management procedures thought likely to produce significant improvements in performance, from operation of the main delivery system to the farm-level. This work would be expected to be of value in two ways: as a source of information which would increase our general understanding about certain principles and relationships affecting the quality of irrigation management; and as an immediate and specific demonstration of what can be achieved by improved management techniques in the particular locality concerned.

This would lead on to the final stage of establishing a national training programme, of which the "demonstration" project would be a major component. The ultimate object would be to develop the capabilities of local officials and researchers to the point at which all responsibilities for training and research in the irrigation field could be handed over entirely to them.

APPENDIX A

Characteristics of irrigation projects and their effect on management skills required (with special reference to water allocation and maintenance)

Table 1. Two projects with contrasting characteristics

Project A (New project: Years 1-5):

(i)   Storage capacity: reduced variability in seasonal water supplies.
(ii)   High technology water delivery system (e.g. automated downstream control).
(iii)   Low rainfall, light soils, even topography.
(iv)   Adequate drainage installed.
(v)   Compact system, designed for high cropping intensities.
(vi)   Regular layout; control structures to field level.
(vii)   No water scarcity (demand lower in initial years of project).
(viii) Control over cropping patterns: single cash crop dominant.
(ix)   High water charges (indirect charges made at point of marketing cash crop).
(x)   Farmers are tenants (with equal plot sizes) under project authority's control.
(xi)   Farmers' technical knowledge low.

Project A (Years 5-10):

The same as in Years 1-5, except for the following changes:
(vii)   Greater water scarcity, owing to increased demand (increased intensity of water use).
(x)   Pressure from farmers for greater autonomy of decision-making (including, e.g. diversification of cropping pattern).
(xi)   Increased technical knowledge.

Project B (Somewhat older project):

(i)   No storage: dependent on diversion of river flows; significant variability in seasonal water supplies.
(ii)   Low technology water delivery system, capable of limited flexibility.
(iii)   High rainfall in concentrated peak periods, heavy soils, broken topography.
(iv)   Drainage required but not installed.
(v)   Extended system, designed for low cropping intensities.
(vi)   Irregular layout; irregular topography; facilities for water control poor.
(vii)   Water scarcity.
(viii) Free choice of cropping.
(ix)   Low water charges (based on area irrigated, not volumetric).
(x)   Poor social cohesion; farm sizes/incomes highly skewed; local politics highly active.
(xi)   Farmers' technical knowledge low.

Table 2A. Requirements of management skills on Project A

Project A (Years 1-5):

(i)   Skills required in reservoir management (planning optimal pattern of water releases).
(ii) High demands on engineering skills and supervisory/training skills at top level; good technical back-up staff for maintenance (particularly on mechanical repair side); low demands on unskilled operators; low demands on staff for reporting up-stream about supply and demand for water (information function).
(iii) Low demands on staff for maintenance of earthworks and canal roads; water supply calculations not complicated by rainfall.
(iv) Only routine maintenance required.
(v)   No special demands on water allocation skills (as long as (vii) below applies); but high potential returns to intensive agricultural extension.
(vi) Quantity of water supplied easily checked; equity of water distribution easily controlled; simple routine procedures required for irrigation staff.
(vii) No particular water allocation skills required.
(viii) Simplifies water allocation function skill further; but seasonal peak demands may need to be evened out by staggering of farming operations on an area-by-area basis—calling for technical (agronomic) expertise (e.g. use of longer/shorter duration crop varieties) and high level of administrative skills in organizing rotation of farming operations, organizing input supplies, etc.
(ix) Need for administrative control over water use and allocation further reduced (cf. (vi) above); and indirect charges (by deduction at point of marketing) require no special revenue-collecting agencies.
(x)   Problems of conflict with farmers or with outside political influence relatively minor.
(xi) Need for good agricultural and water management extension staff.

Project A (Years 5-10):

The same as in Years 1-5, except for the following changes:
(vii) Increased need for water allocation skills on the part of irrigation staff.
(x)   Increased need for two-way information flow instead of merely one-way: need for local (and federated?) irrigators' associations to facilitate discussion; increased need for more complex farm management (i.e. economic) skills on agricultural extension side.
(xi) Possibility for greater delegation of certain functions to farmers; extension staff with fewer purely supervisory functions can concentrate more on farm management/planning functions (cf. (x) above).

Table 2B. Requirement of management skills on Project B

Project B:

(i)   Need for high level of skills in relating pattern of supply as closely as possible to pattern of demand, especially in combination with (vii) and (viii); demands good information flows from field to head and close coordination between engineers (working on water scheduling) and agriculturalists (working on alternative cropping patterns).
(ii) Low demands on sophisticated engineering or maintenance skills; high demands on semi-skilled and unskilled O & M staff and on establishment of clear work routines and close supervision by senior staff; high demands on transport for supervisory tasks.
(iii) High periodic demands for maintenance of earthworks, roads, structures; water supply calculations affected by rainfall and therefore high returns to capacity to improvise water scheduling patterns.
(iv) Need for particular care in controlling water supply patterns and water use, to avoid waterlogging and salinity.
(v)   Because water has to be spread thinly, choice of cropping pattern is likely to be reduced; this may simplify estimation of water demand (but at the same time increase returns to imaginative farm management planning and advice); size of system increases problems of communication each way: therefore good telecommunications essential.
(vi) Problems of water discipline increased (especially in combination with (x)).
(vii) See (i) above.
(viii) See (i) and (v) above.
(ix) Increased demands on control over efficiency of water use at farm level by administrative/technical means (cf. (x) below). Implies high administrative costs per water charges recovered.
(x)   Project authorities require strong legal and political backing to enforce water discipline: also extensive "police force".
(xi) Need for good agricultural and water management extension staff.

REFERENCES

Ali, M. F. Performance of Ganges-Kobadak project (Bangladesh), Paper to *ODI Workshop on Choices in Irrigation Management*, Canterbury, (September 1976).

Biggs, S., Edwards, C. and Griffith, J. *Irrigation in Bangladesh: On Contradictions and Underutilised Potential*, IDS, Sussex, (April 1977) Mimeo.

Birkelbach, A. W. The Subak Association, *Indonesia*, **16**, 153-169 (1973).

Bos, M. B. and Nugteren, J. *On Irrigation Efficiencies*, Wageningen, (1974).

Carruthers, I., Clayton, E. and Hamawi, F. Wadi Dhuleil Jordan: An ex-post evaluation, Occasional Paper No. 1, Wye College, (December 1974).

Chambers, R. and Moris, J. *Mwea: an Irrigated Rice Settlement in Kenya*, Weltforum Verlag, Munchen, (1973).

Chambers, R. *The Organisation and Operation of Irrigation: An Analysis of Evidence from S. India and Sri Lanka*, Centre of South Asian Studies, Cambridge, (1974) Mimeo.

Chambers, R. Water management and paddy production in the dry land zone of Sri Lanka, Agrarian Research and Training Institute, Colombo, Occasional Paper No. 8, (January 1975).

Clay, E. *Adaptive Technology and Participation in Agricultural Innovation: A Case Study of Tubewell Irrigation in N.E. India,* Falmer, UK, IDS, Sussex, (1972).

Coward, E. W. *Irrigation Institutions and Organisations: An International Bibliography*, Department of Rural Sociology, Cornell University, (January 1976).

Dommen, A. The bamboo tubewell: a note on an example of indigenous technology, *Econ. Dev. Cult. Change*, **23** (3), 483-489, (1975).

Geertz, C. Tihingan: a Balinese village, in *Villages in Indonesia*, Koentjarangingrat (ed.) Cornell, (1967).

Harriss, J. *Problems of Water Management in Relation to Social Organisation in Hambantota District*, Centre of South Asian Studies, Cambridge, (December 1974) Mimeo.

Levine, G. The management component in irrigation system design and operation, *Agric. Admin.*, **4** (1) (January 1977).

Mellor, J. W. and Moorti, T. V. Dilemma of state tubewells, *Polit. Econ. Wkly,* **VI**, 13, (March 27, 1971).

Moris, J. R. *The Transferability of Western Management Concepts and Programs, an East African Perspective*, Bellagio Conference on Public Administration and Training, (August 1976) Mimeo.

Motooka, T. *Agricultural Development in Thailand*, Center of South East Asian Studies, University of Kyoto, Vol. III, (no date).

Reidinger, R. B. Institutional rationing of canal water in N. India: conflict between traditional patterns and modern needs, *Econ. Dev. Cult. Change*, **23** (1) (October 1974).

Stoner R. F. Conjunctive use of surface and groundwater supplies, Paper to *ODI Workshop on Choices in Irrigation Management*, Canterbury, (September 1976).

Taylor, D. C. and Pasandaran, E. The management of irrigation systems in the Pekalen Sampean Irrigation Project, East Java, Indonesia, Agro Economic Survey, Research Note No. 01/76/RN, (22 March 1976).

Valera, A. and Wickham, T. Management of traditional and improved irrigation systems: some findings from the Philippines, Paper to *ODI Workshop on Choices in Irrigation Management*, Canterbury, (September 1976).

Vohra, B. B. *Land and Water Management Problems in India*, Training Division, Department of Personnel and Administrative Reforms, Cabinet Secretariat, New Delhi, Training Vol. 8, (March 1975).

Wade, R. Rationing water: principles and practice in South India, Paper to *ODI Workshop on Choices in Irrigation Management*, Canterbury, (September 1976).

Zabala, R. Chimborazo irrigation district Ecuador, Paper to *ODI Workshop on Choices in Irrigation Management*, Canterbury, (September 1976).

Water Supply & Management, Vol. 2, pp. 333-340.
© Pergamon Press Ltd., 1978. Printed in Great Britain.

0364-7714/78/0801-0333$02.00/0

Management of Rural Water Supplies

GUNNAR SCHULTZBERG

The status of domestic water supplies in developing countries has recently become a matter of deep national and international concern. The UN Habitat conference (1976) in Vancouver, Canada, adopted a resolution which aimed at universal service coverage by 1990 in both rural and urban areas. The UN Water Conference in Mar del Plata, Argentina, last year, confirmed the Habitat target and recommended that 1981-1990 be declared a Drinking Water Supply and Sanitation Decade.

The Economic and Social Council of the UN has subsequently requested a report on the implications of the target and WHO has been asked to be the lead Agency in the preparation of this report.

The meeting of the target is a gigantic task. In a survey undertaken by WHO in 1975 of 75 developing countries with a total population of about 2 billion, it was estimated that about 1.2 billion did not have access to a reasonably adequate domestic water supply. Of the unserved population 90% were defined as rural. It is therefore clear that the major attention will have to be directed towards the rural sub-sector. The rural population served in the above 75 countries was estimated at 300 million; between now and 1990 the rural population increase in the same countries will exceed 400 million.

I have been asked to talk on the subject of Management of Rural Water Supplies and will discuss some of the issues related to the planning, development and operation of the national rural water supply programmes and will also make a short review of the role of external aid agencies in this sector.

PLANNING AND POLICY ISSUES

Institutional framework

Rural water supply programmes have, in most developing countries, emerged from the ministries of health in their efforts to prevent water-borne and water-related diseases. In many countries, particularly in Latin America and South Asia, the development of domestic water supplies has remained with the health ministries whereas the rural programme in some countries has been transferred to the agency responsible for urban water supplies, which means that better use is made of available manpower resources. This is the case in Kenya, Tanzania and Ghana for instance. In some countries domestic rural water supply is looked upon as a complementary to integrated rural development programmes and the responsibility rests with the Minister of Agriculture. It is very common that several ministries are active in the rural water supply sector; frequently without defined areas of responsibility, leading to uncoordinated planning and execution of projects. Malawi appears to be an exception. Progress has been excellent in the past few years in spite of the fact that the responsibility is split between three ministries: Community Development and Social Welfare, Agriculture and Natural Resources, and Health.

It does not appear that any particular institutional arrangement is the most appropriate. There are successes and failures in all the models although as a rule fragmentation of sector responsibility leads to duplication and less than optimum use of scarce resources.

The national political will, the motivation of the potential beneficiaries and the ability of the agency to work with the people are factors of importance that overshadow the institutional model.

Government agencies operate under varying degrees of decentralization. There are certain functions that cannot be decentralized, such as:

preparation of national plans and budgets;
allocation of funds;
development of standards for design, construction and operation;
procurement of imported material;
manpower development; and
evaluation.

The degree of decentralization of responsibility for design and construction depends on the size of the country, the availability of manpower, communication facilities and technology utilized.

Responsibility for operation and maintenance has to be decentralized. In very large countries such as India, Nigeria and Pakistan, the development programmes are planned and executed at state or provincial level. Tanzania, which is a much smaller country, works according to a similar model. The delegation of responsibility to the 18 regions has gone so far that the central ministry has almost lost the overall picture and can hardly fulfil the necessary central functions. The system is extremely difficult to manage due to the scarcity of competent national staff that can implement the regional programmes. The development work in Kenya is in contrast very much centralized with even weaker provincial organizations, with the exception of the Coast province.

Target setting

Many countries do not have a national target and clearly defined policies for rural water supply development. They have a project-by-project approach, often steered by what external financial and technical resources they can attract for their programme.

There are a number of variables to be taken into account in the formulation of national programmes, such as:

priority areas and selection of schemes;
level of service to be provided; and
participation of the potential beneficiaries and their contribution towards the programme.

Priority areas and selection of schemes—Ideally one would wish to base scheme selection on benefit-cost analyses. It is extremely difficult to identify which changes have occurred as a result of the introduction of a rural water supply in an evaluation exercise, and it is even more difficult to quantify the benefits in terms of money. In the selection process one deals with potential benefits. The only analyses that can be carried out with any degree of accuracy is cost effectiveness analyses and to make a comparison between the traditional source available in case of alternative schemes proposed. Everything else being equal, it is obvious that schemes with the lowest *per capita* cost should be selected first.

The availability and reliability of health statistics is as a rule so poor that with the exception of areas with cholera epidemics they do not give a good indication of where people are in the greatest need of an improved water supply from a health point of view.

It is quite common for areas selected for integrated rural development projects to be given first priority in the rural water supply programmes. The water component has a catalytic effect and enables economic and social benefits to be realized.

The selection of rural water projects generally follows one of three models, namely:

(i)   centralized selection based on primarily political criteria;
(ii) scheme proposals reviewed and screened by development committees at various levels with emphasis on technical, cost and political criteria;
(iii) schemes selected in response to requests from villages and their willingness to contribute towards the development and operation and maintenance in a major consideration in the selection.

There appears to be a distinct relationship between a genuine commitment on the part of the villages selected and the success of programmes. In several Latin American countries with successful rural water supply programmes, full time promoters whose task is to motivate the people, are engaged.

Level of service—The most debated component of national policy formulation is probably the question of level of service to be provided in terms of quantity and quality of water and proximity to the consumers.

The major benefit aimed at in rural water supply development is usually better health for the people. The potential beneficiaries might not see it the same way. What they primarily look for is improved convenience and they are frequently not aware of the relationship between good water and good health. This determines the minimum level of service required for people to use the water service. It is unlikely that they will cross an irrigation ditch or a stream to collect water from a standpost. The water supply must be more convenient than the traditional source. This means that the minimum service level will be a variable as the traditional source varies in convenience.

The more affluent and well-to-do sections of the rural population consider that anything short of a water connection on their plot is not worth contributing to. Should they be left without service until those who are worse off have been served? In some countries, i.e. Tanzania and Malawi, the Government has adopted the policy of not providing any individual connections until the whole population has been provided with a minimum level of service. In Kenya individual service connections are encouraged in high potential areas with the hope of achieving higher economic and health benefits and to facilitate the collection of revenue for the service. In South Korea rural schemes are based on plot connections to all households.

The *per capita* volume of water required may vary from 20 l in systems based on standpost service to up to 100 l where the proportions of house or plot connections is very high.

Water quality standard should be set to provide safe water from a bacteriological point of view.

Consumer participation—The question of level of service is closely linked with the question of consumer participation in the form of cash or kind. In some countries, the provision of water to the rural people is considered a social service to be given free of charge.

A WHO engineer carried out a feasibility study for water supply in some villages in one country a couple of years ago and came to the conclusion that shallow wells with handpumps would be the most appropriate and lowest cost solution. His proposal was not well received by the villagers, he was actually asked to leave. Their argument was that the neighbouring village received water from a deep borehole equipped with a diesel engine and they did not have to do the pumping themselves. Their reaction might have been different had they been charged for the cost of the water service.

PROGRAMME IMPLEMENTATION

Appropriate and low cost technology are words which are frequently used today in connection with aid programmes. Nothing earthshaking has taken place in the field of rural water supplies. The technology to be used is often determined by the physical conditions and the options are limited. There is sometimes a choice between developing a groundwater or surface-water source. Groundwater is generally more reliable from the quality point of view whereas the cost of operation of a gravity supply based on surface-water is considerably lower than the utilization of a pumped groundwater source.

When there is a choice in equipment to be used there is much to be said for selecting the least complex machinery. The logistic support is frequently very inadequate and the actual output of, for instance, complex drilling equipment is usually much below the theoretical values when operated within a government administrative system.

Self-help versus paid labour

Construction work is carried out with paid labourers or with the help of free self-help labour from the potential beneficiaries. The success of self-help requires that the villagers are highly motivated and that there has been some involvement on their part in the selection of the scheme. Utility oriented water supply agencies are generally against self-help labour with the arguments that it slows down construction progress and it makes revenue collection more difficult as the villagers feel that God provides the water and they did the digging, so there is no justification for charges.

Self-help labour can bring down construction costs and as a primary benefit introduce a sense of belonging to the people served.

In the Republic of Korea, which has a very successful rural water supply programme, the whole village is mobilized to build the supply. The average construction period for a supply from a spring to a population of 500-1000 people was reported to be one week.

In Malawi, a number of gravity rural schemes serving large areas and supplying up to 80,000 people have been successfully built with self-help labour and a minimum of ministerial staff. The construction of each scheme is preceded by an extensive period of motivation of the people.

The utilization of consultants and contractors in the implementation of rural water supply programmes makes it possible to accelerate the development in countries where skilled manpower resources are scarce and makes it possible for the government agency to concentrate their manpower development on the operation and maintenance. The drawback is that the scope for involvement of the villagers is more limited.

Piped rural systems are often very much under-utilized in the initial phase and theoretically one can make considerable savings through deferring construction of certain components of the supply (e.g. balancing storage tanks).

The problem is, that when the component is required some years later, it is likely that the limited resources available will be directed towards an area which has received no service yet, rather than to an improvement of an existing scheme.

OPERATION AND MAINTENANCE

Problems related to development are generally small compared to those encountered in the operational phase. Resources required for operation and maintenance are frequently under-estimated in budget proposals and approving authorities usually make considerable reductions of the requests when it comes to actual allocations. Countries are often able to attract external resources for development but usually not for operation and maintenance. SIDA is here an exception in that they have provided budgetary support for maintenance for Tanzania and Kenya.

The problems seem to increase with centralization of the responsibility for operation and maintenance. In most countries it is possible to identify and train people locally for the operation of the systems and where this is done the success rate is higher.

In, for instance, the Republic of Korea and Afghanistan local operators also collect money required for fuel and their own salary from the villagers. In Malawi local operators look after the schemes, no revenue is collected. The schemes are either gravity fed or based on handpumps which means that operating costs are virtually nil. In Tanzania no revenue has been collected so far and facilities are frequently not in use due to lack of diesel for the pumps. In Kenya there are considerable operation problems caused by lack of funds and manpower resources and inadequate administrative procedures for reporting and repairing failures. A non-operating supply deteriorates very quickly as people tend to destroy taps and pumps when they do not deliver the desired water.

In some states of India and also in Malawi the agency responsible for maintenance is informed by a pre-printed post card from the operator about operational problems.

Mobile maintenance teams visit the schemes regularly and make special visits when requested through the post card system.

The financial burden from operation and maintenance is rapidly increasing in those countries which have undertaken rural water supply as a social service. It appears that raising of funds for at least the cost of operation at the local level, is a must, or supplies will be going out of service almost at the same rate as they are being constructed.

MANPOWER DEVELOPMENT

In most developing countries with the exception of India, Bangladesh, Pakistan and, to a certain extent, Latin America, there is considerable competition for staff with technical know-how in the water supply sector. Many prefer to work in the urban sub-sector as it might give more prestige and provide more of a challenge from a technical point of view. It is also true that most of the educated people prefer to work in the cities rather than have to cope with the problems associated with working in the rural areas.

The best solution to ensure availability of staff is probably in-house training by the water supply agencies with courses of a sandwich type where theoretical training is mixed with on the job training.

Some countries, primarily in Africa, rely to a very large extent on expatriates in the planning and execution of their rural water supply programmes. This enables them to proceed with their development programmes although there are problems with discontinuity in many posts due to the quick turnover of the expatriates and delays in the recruitment of replacements.

Volunteers have made very useful contributions to the development programmes. They are prepared to live and work in the rural areas with the people.

EXTERNAL ASSISTANCE

Multilateral and bilateral agencies provide technical and financial assistance to the sector.

WHO has, since its inception, emphasized Environmental Health. Sanitary engineers were initially posted to ministries of health to assist in the development of water and sanitation demonstration projects. The Organization has currently some 150 engineers posted in the field, the majority of them are engaged on environmental health activities in the rural areas. WHO has, over the past 6 years, assisted Governments in the preparation of water supply and sewerage sector studies under a cooperative programme with the World Bank.

UNDP has provided funds for the execution of national studies in rural water supply in Ghana and Iraq.

UNICEF has over the past 15 years been providing construction material for rural water supply programmes and is very active in many countries. As of late they have engaged expertise to provide assistance also in the planning and execution of these programmes and they have now a technical field staff of about 60.

The World Bank has, since Mr. McNamara's speech in Nairobi in 1973, become more and more involved in rural projects. Finance to rural water supplies is provided in the following forms:

(i)   programme loan or credit to an agency responsible for both urban and rural water supplies (e.g. Utter Pradesh in India and Brazil);

(ii) loan or credit to integrated rural development projects (e.g. Kigoma Region in Tanzania);

(iii) direct support of rural water supply projects (not very common, the only one I know of is a package of projects in Kenya which was recently appraised but not yet approved).

Of the regional development banks, the Inter-American Development Bank has so far been the most active.

Bilateral agencies have provided the largest share of external support to the rural water supply sector; Sweden, Canada, USA, the Netherlands and Germany have made the biggest contributions.

International agencies have expressed concern over the slow progress in rural water supply and sanitation development. In 1974 an *ad hoc* Committee for rural water supply and sanitation was formed with the aim of a joint effort. Unfortunately no formula for a collaborative mechanism has as yet been agreed upon.

CONCLUSIONS

The improvement of the rural water supply situation in developing countries is a major challenge. The problems vary between the regions of the world; in Latin America, India, Pakistan, Bangladesh and some countries in the Far East the know-how and manpower resources are available—shortage of funds for development is the major constraint. In the Middle East the situation is almost the opposite, funds are available but not the manpower. Most African countries suffer from shortage of both financial and manpower resources.

The rich countries can help in plugging the gaps, prerequisite for successful programmes is a national commitment towards the sector and that the potential beneficiaries are motivated and prepared to contribute towards the operation and maintenance of constructed facilities so that they will continue to function after they have been installed.

In addition to assistance towards the construction of new facilities, external inputs are often required for:

national planning;
institution building;
water resources studies;
manpower development; and
equipment and facilities required for proper operation and maintenance.

To achieve optimum benefits from rural water supply programmes, complementary inputs are required. From the health point of view, health education and sanitation programmes are required. From the economic point of view, opportunities to use the time saved by the introduction of a more convenient water source need to be created.

Health Aspects of Water Development

"What faith is it that makes us hope that the provision of rural water supplies, or other environmental improvements, will convert poor, deprived, sick children into poor, deprived, healthy children?"

Richard Feachem

Water Supply & Management, Vol. 2, pp. 343-350.
© Pergamon Press Ltd., 1978. Printed in Great Britain.

0364-7714/78/0801-0343$02.00/0

Starvation or Bilharzia?— a Rural Development Dilemma

LETITIA E. OBENG

I have the pleasure to consider a beautiful subject: starvation or bilharzia? I have a similar beautiful answer to the question: neither. Both starvation and bilharzia are undesirable. Neither presents much of a choice. At best they are unhealthy, at worst they are fatal. They are both best avoided. Yet, food is a basic human need and it is indeed true that in certain circumstances, some water intensive agricultural processes undertaken to prevent shortage of food, enhance the incidence of bilharzia (or schistosomiasis), a serious rural malady, by creating habitats for freshwater snails of the genera *Bulinus, Biomphalaria* and *Oncomelania*, the host snails for the three common human schistome parasites. Hence the dilemma. But it should be possible to produce adequate food without the risk of schistosomiasis. The crux of the matter is whether indeed there is the will to do so.

WHAT REALLY IS THE LINK BETWEEN SCHISTOSOMIASIS AND FOOD PRODUCTION?

Schistosomiasis is a worm disease which affects human beings and some animals. The disease is intimately related to freshwater availability for its transmission since the terminal stages of the life cycle of the parasite outside man, and the production of the infective worm take place in freshwater snails. The potential for the spread of the disease is therefore increased by water development projects such as irrigation schemes and artificial impoundments.

When such projects are located in rural regions of low economic development, the chances for the establishment of the disease are increased. In such areas, usually, sanitation is bad, disposal of waste is unsatisfactory, and water sources are easily contaminated with human feces and urine containing the eggs of the schistosome parasites. Water supply also tends to be unsafe and people are in frequent contact with infected waters which very often provide for domestic water. In the course of fishing or farming irrigated lands, people and the parasite come into contact. Especially on impoundments and large-scale irrigation schemes in endemic areas, the contact greatly aids the establishment and spread of the disease.

HOW SERIOUS IS THE DISEASE?

Schistosomiasis is one of the world's oldest known and documented diseases. It plagued the Egyptians for centuries, the parasite eggs being found in Egyptian mummies dating

343

back to the XXth Dynasty (1250-1000 BC). The Nile provided suitable ecological conditions. It was also an established disease in Iraq and Iran which had the Tigris and Euphrates. In China, *S. japonicum* has been identified in the remains of a woman who died in 186 BC. It is relevant and interesting to note that at the time, irrigation was well-developed in these areas—in the food producing valleys of the Nile, Tigris and Euphrates and in the rice paddy fields of China.

At present, schistosomiasis is widespread in tropical and sub-tropical zones in Africa, Japan, Philippines, Thailand, Laos, other parts of Asia, the Middle East, West Indies and parts of South America, and in a total of 71 countries. But this is only the thin edge of the wedge, it can spread to other areas where climatic, ecological, social, cultural and economic conditions favour its establishment.

Currently it affects over 200 million people and many more are liable to infection as in recent years, many water development projects and impoundments have been undertaken and the connection between water/irrigation development and the disease is without question. There are many excellent case studies.

DAMS, IRRIGATION PROJECTS AND SCHISTOSOMIASIS

Centuries ago, the Khuzestan Province of Iran was very fertile. As far back as 3000 BC, irrigation schemes had been established and the area produced abundant food. With the collapse of the Darius Empire around 300 BC and the subsequent troubles, the canal and irrigation systems fell into disuse, but they were reconstructed much later and the area again flourished. By the 16th Century however, the area had lost its fertility and the land was uncultivated. In 1961, the Iranian Government initiated a pilot irrigation project in the Khuzestan and by 1975, water was once again flowing in the area and with it, arose the hope of abundant food. But with this also came widespread schistosomiasis.

Another slightly different example is the history of the disease in Egypt. For centuries, the Nile flood waters had been used for irrigation, but when irrigation was carried out on a continuous basis the schistosomiasis prevalance picture changed. Lanoix (1958) indicates that the population infected with schistosomiasis increased, in one study from as low as 2% to 75% when irrigation was introduced to some areas in Egypt (Table 1).

Table 1. Prevalence of schistosomiasis before and after introduction of irrigation in parts of Egypt

Area	Percentage of infection	
	1934	1937
Sibaia	10	44
Kilh	7	50
Mansouria	11	64
Binban	2	75

With the completion of the Aswan High Dam, the seasonal flooding of the Nile Valley was controlled, water was stored and it became constantly available. In more areas, the periodic irrigation that had previously been practiced changed to continuous or perennial irrigation to increase food production. With the continuous irrigation, schistosomiasis which already existed, became more widespread with an estimated infection rate of 100% in some rural communities.

The story is similar in many rural areas in Asia where peasant irrigation is practiced to produce rice, and in Africa and other areas where limited or large-scale irrigation is undertaken.

Irrigation schemes are not the only channels for the spread of the disease. Man-made water impoundments which also provide water for irrigation and fish production, cause drastic ecological changes which, in endemic areas, enhance conditions for the spread of schistosomiasis. The artifical lakes which have been built in Africa in recent decades provide a basis for interesting studies. On all of them, (but Lakes Nasser and Volta especially) in varying degrees, transmission sites have been created and infection rates have soared.

In other instances, quiet reaches of rivers can be transmission sites. Contact with such areas in the course of fishing, farming and other forms of agriculture in fertile river valleys and lake basins have been a constant source of infection with schistosomiasis. It may here be mentioned as a matter of interest that there are other diseases which also have an impact on food production. In West Africa, fertile valleys have been abandoned because of the bite of the blackfly, *Simulium damnosum* which breeds in fast rivers. This fly transmits the worm parasite *Onchocerca volvulus* which causes river blindness. The people are forced to farm in safer, but less fertile areas. Malaria, dengue fever and even the mere population explosion of mayflies in river basins have also been known to threaten the continued occupation of some areas.

Since starvation cannot be accepted, the matter under discussion therefore reduces to how to produce food without becoming infected with schistosomiasis.

One fact has to be firmly recognized. It should not be taken for granted that once there is irrigation, schistosomiasis is inevitable. There is at present, ample knowledge, technical experience and effective methods available for planning and designing irrigation schemes and taking adequate precautions to control the spread of schistosomiasis. However, there are still some difficulties in achieving the level of safety required. Before examining some of these control measures, it is necessary to remind ourselves of the disease schistosomiasis and the factors which promote its spread.

SCHISTOSOMES AND THEIR LIFE CYCLE

Schistosomiasis is caused by species of parasitic flatworms of the genus *Schistosoma*. There are three common species which infect man: *S. haematobium*, *S. mansoni* and *S. japonicum*. Schistosomes are so called because the sides of the body of the adult male fold over towards the middle to form a groove which gives it a "split" appearance. Each worm is either male or female. The larval stages develop in intermediate freshwater snail hosts and the adult worm lives in man where it matures, mates and produces eggs.

The eggs of the human schistosomes, which for each species are characteristically spined, escape from the human body via the urine or feces. The eggs are 70-170 μm long by 40-70 μm wide and under suitable conditions, may be viable for up to a month. In water, due to changes in osmotic pressure, the eggs hatch to release the free-living ciliated larva, the miracidium, which has a life span of only 24 hr. Within this time, it must find and penetrate a suitable intermediate host snail or perish. *S. japonicum* develops in *Oncomelania* spp., *S. mansoni* in *Biomphalaria* (also *Australorbis* spp.) and *S. haematobium* in *Bulinus* spp.

In the snail, the miracidium undergoes development into another larval form, the sporocyst, which within 4-8 weeks, asexually produces thousands of the infective fork-tailed larva, the cercaria. Each is microscopic in size, being only up to 0.5 mm long, and generally not visible *in situ*, in nature. It can live for 24-72 hr, after which time it dies unless it finds the final host, which is man.

Upon contact with man, the cercariae bore through the skin in minutes, enter the blood circulation system within hours, and move to the liver where they grow to maturity in a few weeks and then mate. The female enters the mating groove of the male and stays there permanently. Adult *S. mansoni* and *S. japonicum* settle down and literally become egg-producing machines, turning out many eggs a day for the whole life time of the worm which is believed to last for up to 35 years! With such a fantastic multiplication system, it is little wonder that there are so many infective cercariae in waters at transmission sites to attack unsuspecting victims.

Similarly, *S. haematobium* stays in the branches of the vesical vein and produces eggs. The entire cycle from one egg stage to the other is just over 14 weeks, of which about 8 weeks is spent in the definitive host and 4 weeks in the intermediate host. Without re-infection it should theoretically be possible to control *S. haematobium* and cure people. However, in endemic areas—where the problem exists—people tend to be exposed to multiple and continuous infections.

WHAT HARM DOES THE DISEASE DO TO MAN?

Schistosomiasis caused by *S. japonicum* is severe and generally fatal. In the urinary and intestinal forms of the disease, *S. mansoni* and *S. haematobium* make their impact by weakening patients, depriving them of the ability to work and causing economic losses and social distress to the community. In some cases, death has been directly attributed to the disease, but generally death results from other disease agents using the infection to their advantage.

CLINICAL MANIFESTATION AND PATHOLOGY

Following skin penetration by the cercariae, there is a mild to severe itch within hours of contact with the infected water. Rise in temperature, fever, nausea and vomiting have been recorded within days. In cases of *S. mansoni* and *S. japonicum*, watery and bloody diarrhea, mild cough, enlargement of lymph nodes, spleen and liver follow as the disease progresses. With *S. haematobium*, lesions eventually develop in the bladder and some urinogenital organs. There is fever, general weakness and lassitude and bloody urine rather than bloody diarrhea is usual.

Much of the harm done to the patient is due to toxic substances produced by his own tissues in reaction to the worms. When the worms mature, the extrusion of their eggs also causes tissue damage and bleeding. Eventually, body reaction results in limiting the movement of the eggs which then become embedded in tissues or block passages. Generally, in chronic cases, the disease is accompanied by liver cirrhosis and splenomegaly. The adults of *S. japonicum* generally reside in the terminal veins of the superior mesenteric vein but they are also found in the inferior mesenteric vein and in the extremities of the portal vein within the liver. Similarly, *S. mansoni* primarily inhabits the small veins of the mesenteric vein but may also be in the superior mesenteric vein and within the liver. With *S. haematobium*, the adults are found in the vesical plexus and in the vessels around the rectum. Rarely are they found in the portal vein.

In addition, following autopsies, the eggs of all three species have been reported from various organs. Eggs of *S. japonicum* have been recovered from the brain, and those of *S. mansoni* and *S. haematobium* from the spinal cord. In a study by Shaw (1938), of 282 autopsies of schistosomiasis cases in Egypt, infection of the lungs with ova was recorded in 33% of the cases, and in 2% of the cases the infection was the immediate cause of death. As the schistosome ova are extruded from the vascular system and become trapped because they have no other means of leaving the lungs, tubercles are produced which are similar to those found in cases of pulmonary tuberculosis. The eggs of *S. mansoni* and *S. haematobium* have also been found in the bladder, appendix, rectum, uterus, spleen, liver, lungs and brain.

ECONOMIC IMPACT OF SCHISTOSOMIASIS

It is difficult to quantify accurately, the economic losses due to schistosomiasis and there is little analytical information. Farooq (1963) stated economic losses in the Philippines to be about $6.5 million per yr. He based this loss estimate on the cost of medical attention as well as on the decrease of the patients productivity. He also estimated the economic loss in Egypt to be about $560 million per yr.

Wright (1968) writes: "The latest available figure of *per capita* gross national product for Egypt is $139 and that for Africa except for Egypt is $135. If one assumes then that the 2.1 per cent of persons who have schistosomiasis with heavy clinical involvement are totally disabled, the annual monetary loss for Africa as a whole from this single factor would be approximately 212 million dollars." These figures, which he explained do not include cost of medical treatment and public health programmes, etc., perhaps represent only the potential loss.

Socio-economic effects of schistosomiasis have not been assessed. There is a dearth of knowledge and therefore a need to investigate and assess the impact of schistosomiasis in this sector. What is known is that infection with schistosomiasis produces ill-health. Infected people may continue to work on irrigation schemes but they do not produce at full level and they also become carriers.

IRRIGATION SCHEMES AND SNAIL HABITATS

As regards food production, irrigation is an essential activity though invariably it produces suitable ecological habitats for the snail hosts. *Bulinus* spp. seem to prefer stagnant or slow moving water, especially where there is a good supply of organic matter. But they may also be found elsewhere in permanent or seasonal waters. *Biomphalaria* spp. are generally found in water which is somewhat faster. Sometimes, the snails live in water sources which are not related to agriculture. *Oncomelania* is operculated and amphibious and therefore happy both on land and in water and can stand periods of drying. It is found in swampy irrigation systems, such as oriental rice fields and similar places.

In irrigated agriculture therefore, the extension of snail habitats depends considerably on the form of irrigation system used. The basin and flood types of irrigation favour the establishment and propagation of snails. Canal irrigation also provides suitable habitats especially if the system is not adequately managed as weeds which develop, favour the snails. Sprinkler irrigation, when efficiently applied, can reduce the quantity of irrigation water and the chances of creating habitats for the snails. But, like drip irrigation, it is expensive. The drip method also has other serious setbacks such as the tendency to increase soil salinity. Storage impoundments, irrigation canals and drainage systems all provide potential snail supporting areas. It would seem then, that in our present state of knowledge and technological experience in irrigation, food production also favours the establishment of host snails and the spread of schistosomiasis. This is also because human waste disposal systems and sanitation tend to be unsatisfactory and irrigation water becomes inoculated with the parasite.

CONTROL

An important question then is this: Considering various difficulties, is it worth trying to control schistosomiasis? After all, schistosomiasis does not produce epidemics and to those in non-endemic areas it is only a disease of the poor rural people in some far away place. It is true that the disease does not get the international attention and support for control and cure that it deserves. But, even without accurate analyses, the financial losses that have been linked to schistosomiasis would indicate that some control action should be undertaken. More important still, as with such diseases, the matter of control is not so much one of economic or financial loss as it is the desirable impact that it would make on health and the improvement of life quality.

However, taking only the economic losses into account and comparing, for instance, the estimate of McMullen (1962) (up to $16 million per yr) with the annual loss of $560 million estimated by Farooq, it would seem that control can be justified. Besides, a life which is suffused with ill-health and disease is not really worth living. The benefits which come out of control of schistosomiasis—the absence of pain, the peace of mind, the ability to undertake vigorous action—are all priceless, but they cannot be measured in economic terms. Furthermore, food is a necessity for life and in the interest of sound management and the preservation of man and his environment, we have to make food production and the processes which contribute to it safe.

INTEGRATED CONTROL OF SCHISTOSOMIASIS

Control of the schistosomiasis may be achieved by breaking the life cycle of the parasite at one stage or another. The integrated approach to control, advocates a combination of measures for interrupting transmission and destroying the parasite.

For decades, and even to the present day, the main method of control has been to kill host snails with a variety of molluscicides. Such a control measure however, when undertaken on its own, needs frequent repetition. The chemicals used range from simple to complex synthetic compounds which are also toxic to animals other than the snails. Although they swiftly destroy the snails, one of the biggest drawbacks to the use of molluscicides is the rapid re-establishment of snail populations. There is also the hard fact that molluscicides are too expensive for the poor afflicted countries to afford. Chemicals of plant origin are also known to be snail killers, but we need to know much more about them to be able to put them to effective and safe use.

Another method is the use of biological controls to attack the host snails. The best-known biological control example for schistosomiasis is the use of *Marisa cornuarietis* which has successfully controlled *Australorbis* spp., host snail of *S. mansoni* in Puerto Rico. However, it is still to be proved effective on a large scale elsewhere. Biological control methods using ducks, fishes, etc. in general have not been sufficiently effective to cope with the scale of the problem.

Similarly, other measures used individually have not been fully successful. However, China provides an example of a country which has been successful in the control of schistosomiasis by the use of an integrated approach. The disease is of no serious consequence in a country where 100 million people were previously exposed to it. In a national programme, a number of control measures were combined. Human waste disposal systems were made safe so that feces and urine no longer reached the water resources (canals, rice fields, etc.) Water supply systems were improved so that the people did not come into contact with infected water sources. Snail habitats were destroyed physically by draining extensively where necessary and by filling in transmission sites, etc. The snails themselves were destroyed by burning and burying them and by mechanically removing them. Where necessary, molluscicides were used on a limited scale for mopping up. At the same time infected people were treated to destroy the parasites. Perhaps the most important part of this multi-prong attack on schistosomiasis was the massive public education and mobilization to participate in the control programme. Children assisted the adults in snail destruction. The old prepared tea for them, the doctors attended patients, laboratories undertook research and it was truly a national joint action which paid off.

Perhaps what the Chinese did cannot be directly transferred elsewhere, but the technology is there. Similar measures have been practiced in some instances but they need to be made more effective. In addition to fighting the parasite outside the human body, the search is going on for suitable drugs to attack it inside the body. At present the drugs that exist can neither be conveniently mass-administered nor are they entirely safe.

There are still a number of fundamental questions that need to be answered. For instance, what is the threshold of infection that causes disease? Can treatment be limited to reducing the number of parasites or should all parasites be destroyed before treatment is achieved?

Can the body tissues be sentisized to minimize reaction to the presence of the worms? These questions are still largely unsolved and the search is still going on.

Let us look again at the question under discussion—bilharzia or starvation? We must produce food, but we must also plan and design well to prevent host snails becoming established. This would involve the provision of good sanitation and safe human waste disposal on the schemes to guard against the ova of the parasites infecting the irrigation water. The effective action is satisfactory planning, establishment and management of food production schemes which depend on water use with great care, especially when they are set up in endemic areas.

It is generally difficult to take suitable precautions on such schemes simply because it is very expensive. It is usually easier to take the easy way out and not take the precautions. Satisfactory food production schemes require the attention of all concerned.

Control of schistosomiasis depends on the sense of responsibility and the will to do the right thing—especially by the exposed people. They need the discipline to observe and practice strict sanitation; irrigation and other food producing schemes should be made ecologically safe through efficient management; governments should assist with better water supply systems in rural areas and effective waste disposal everywhere; and the international community and countries not exposed to the diseases should feel the responsibility and have the will to assist with control.

The dilemma is not insoluble: with the will and the commitment of all to "do the right things", rural starvation may be prevented, and the spread of bilharzia curtailed.

REFERENCES

Farooq, M. A possible approach to the evolution of the economic burden imposed on a community by Schistosomiasis, *Ann. Trop. Med. Parasit.*, **57**, 323-331 (1963).

Lanoix, J. N. Relation between irrigation engineering and Bilharziasis, *Bull. Wld Hlth Org.*, **18**, 1011-1035 (1958).

McMullen, D. B. The modification of habitats in the control of Bilharziasis with special reference to water resources development in Bilharziasis, Wolstenholme, G. E. W. and O'Connor, M. (eds) Little Brown, Boston, (1962) pp. 382-396.

Wright, W. H. Schistosomiasis as a world problem, *Bull. N.Y. Acad. Med.*, **44** (3), 301-312 (March 1968).

Water Supply & Management, Vol. 2, pp. 357-362.
© Pergamon Press Ltd., 1978. Printed in Great Britain.

0364-7714/78/0801-0351$02.00/0

Domestic Water Supplies, Health and Poverty

A brief review

RICHARD FEACHEM

Over the past decade, and particularly since the publication in 1972 of the book *Drawers of Water* (White *et al.*, 1972), great interest has focused upon the provision of adequate domestic water supplies for the many hundreds of millions of people who now lack these facilities. It has become clear, following the compilation of statistics by the World Health Organisation (Subrahmanyam, 1977; WHO, 1973, 1976), that the magnitude of the problem is immense and that progress at present is slow. Despite, or because of this, many governments and agencies have pledged themselves to provide an adequate domestic water supply for large numbers of people. The United Nations, first at the Habitat Conference (Vancouver) and later at the Water Conference (Mar del Plata), has set a target of providing all the world's population with an adequate domestic water supply by 1990. Some of the dangers inherent in setting an over-ambitious target of this kind have been recently discussed (Cairncross and Feachem, 1977).

Why is it that so much interest and activity has been focused on domestic water supplies? There are a number of reasons (Feachem *et al.*, 1978) but one of them is certainly that improved domestic water supplies hold out the hope of improved health. It is this promise of improved health, for the millions who currently suffer a heavy burden of infectious disease, which provides much of the stimulus for the massive improvements in domestic water supplies which are now under way.

This goal, of improved health through improved water, has led to a considerable number of investigations and publications on exactly how and why water supplies improve health. These questions, of how and why water supplies improve health or how and why, in some circumstances, water supplies do not improve health, are the subject of this brief paper.

ENVIRONMENTAL TAXONOMY

The fundamental prerequisite for any understanding of water supplies and health is a sound classification of the water-related infections. This classification should not follow

Acknowledgements.—I am indebted to David Bradley, John Briscoe, Sandy Cairncross, Peter Hawkins, Michael Merson, Duncan Mara, Henry Mosley, Mujiber Rahaman and Wilfredo Reyes, who have stimulated my thinking on this subject.

the traditional medical practice of grouping diseases according to the biology of their pathogens, but should group diseases according to the manner in which they are related to water. This, I call an environmental taxonomy of water-related diseases.

A suitable environmental taxonomy was proposed by Bradley and Emurwon (1968) and later used extensively in *Drawers of Water* (White *et al.*, 1972). It was later modified (Feachem, 1975a, 1977a, 1977b) and used in various methodological and practical contexts (Cairncross *et al.*, 1978; Feachem *et al.*, 1978).

The details and rationale of this taxonomy of water-related diseases are fully set out in the publications referred to above. Infectious water-related diseases are divied into four major groups as follows:

1. *Fecal-oral diseases*: (e.g. cholera, typhoid, diarrheas, dysenteries, hepatitis, ascariasis) These are all infections transmitted by the fecal-oral (feco-oral, ano-oral and also fecal-nasal and feco-ocular) route. They may be water-borne or water-washed.
2. *Water-washed diseases*: (e.g. infections of the skin and infections of the eyes) These are all infections related to poor hygiene (therefore water-washed) but which are not fecal-oral and are not water-borne.
3. *Water-based diseases*: (e.g. guinea worm, schistosomiasis, clonorchiasis) These are all the helminths which have an aquatic intermediate host.
4. *Water-related insect vector*: (e.g. malaria, filariases, yellow fever, trypanosomiasis (Gambian only)) These are all infections transmitted by insects which either breed in water or bite near water.

It will be clear to the reader that the terms "water-borne" and "water-washed" are being used in precise ways. Water-borne transmission occurs when the pathogen is drunk in polluted water. Water-washed transmission occurs when the pathogen is passed from man to man by a route which reflects poor personal or domestic hygiene and therefore which might be controlled by the use of more water as an aid to hygiene. Water-borne transmission is thus related to *water quality* while water-washed transmission relates to *water quantity*.

This taxonomy is set out in more detail elsewhere and its use is discussed in Cairncross *et al.* (1978) and Feachem (1977b) and demonstrated in Feachem (1977c) and Feachem *et al.* (1978). See also Duguid *et al.* (1976) for interesting date on feco-ocular infection of mice with *Salmonella typhimurium*. See also Moore (1957).

INVESTIGATIONS INTO WATER SUPPLIES AND HEALTH

Over the past 25 years there have been a number of field studies into the impact on health of domestic water supplies. Some of these have recently been reviewed (Saunders and Warford, 1976). Since this review was published, other detailed studies have appeared, including a series of studies on cholera, shigellosis and water supplies in Bangladesh conducted by the Cholera Research Laboratory (for instance, Curlin *et al.*, 1977 and Levine *et al.*, 1976), and a study of water supplies and water-related disease in Lesotho (Feachem *et al.*, 1978). The Bangladesh studies have been recently reviewed by Briscoe (1977). I will not attempt another full review of these studies here but will rather give a brief summary of the main outcome.

There has been a widespread, although not universal, tendency to fail to demonstrate any marked association between water quality and diarrheal disease. For instance, Moore *et al.* (1965) concluded in Costa Rica that "water pollution could not be shown to have a direct effect upon diarrhea morbidity". Feachem *et al.* (1978) failed to find an association between water supplies of improved quality and diarrheal disease or typhoid in Lesotho, while Levine *et al.* (1976) failed to demonstrate an association between the incidence of cholera and other diarrheas and the use of tubewells in Bangladesh. Other examples could be cited in which improvements in water quality were not clearly associated with a reduction in fecal-oral diseases. There are a few possible explanations for this, one of which is that, in the communities studied, the fecal-oral diseases under consideration were not *primarily* water-borne but were transmitted *mainly* by other routes. Another possible explanation is that, in the communities studied, the people with the highest prevalance of diarrheal disease (namely small children) were not using the improved water supply in the same way as adults (Briscoe, 1977). This point will be discussed at greater length below.

A second theme which emerges from these studies is that the provision of public taps in a community may not in itself change hygiene or water use patterns and may not even increase the volume of water used *per capita*. Some studies have even found that bringing the water source substantially closer to, but not into, the house may not increase the volume of water used (White *et al.*, 1972; Feachem, 1973; Feachem *et al.*, 1978).

A third theme is that where the availability of water is greatly improved, and particularly where communal washing or laundry facilities or house connections are provided, a marked reduction in water-related disease may be found. This has been found, for instance, with shigellosis in California (Hollister *et al.*, 1955) and with schistosomiasis in St Lucia (Jordan *et al.*, 1975).

However, it is perhaps the first theme, namely the lack of association between water quality and health, which is of most importance and this will be further discussed in the next section.

A RECIPE FOR FAILURE

Let us now examine what may happen when a water supply is built and consider the probable impact on health. I will present a caricature of a village water supply project which I believe to be typical of water installations in many countries—especially in Africa.

A village of 400 people used to take its water from two hand-dug wells on the edge of the village. The water in these wells was heavily contaminated and the wells had no head-wall to prevent surface water from draining into them. In some dry seasons the wells would dry up and the villagers would then walk considerable distances to collect water from temporary wells dug in the bed of a dry river. In this village a new water supply is constructed as part of the government's rural water supply programme. This new supply might be tubewells with hand pumps; or it might be a boxed spring with gravity supply to public taps; or it might be a diesel or wind pumped supply from a borehole to a tank and from there gravity feed to public taps. Whatever the exact design, the new construction leads to public water sources in the village at about one source per 100 people and the water supplied, although probably not treated, is of good microbiological quality.

Supposing that this supply is well operated and maintained (which is often not the case; Cairncross and Feachem, 1977), let us examine what changes it has brought to the

Fig. 1. An improved well in Northern Nigeria. Water in such a well will probably be fecally polluted and may contribute to the transmission of water-borne infection (Photo: R. G. Feachem).

community. It has improved water quality very substantially. It has brought water closer to houses, especially in the dry season, and has thus considerably improved water availability. However, in some areas (Feachem, 1973; Feachem *et al.*, 1978; White *et al.*, 1972) people will not use more water simply because it is closer. The water supply, if accompanied by no health education campaign, is unlikely to change hygiene or water use and storage practices. Therefore, life goes on just as before. Hygiene is the same; water use is the same; the only change is that before the women walked to a polluted well and now they walk a shorter distance to collect clean water from a tap.

The only effect on health of such an installation will be to reduce the *water-borne* transmission of the fecal-oral group of diseases and to eliminate guinea worm transmission occurring at the water source. Assuming that the community does not have endemic guinea worm, this leaves only the *water-borne component* of the fecal-oral group as being affected. Groups 2, 3 and 4 will be unchanged. Clearly, if the fecal-oral disease in the community is largely transmitted by non-water-borne fecal-oral routes—as may be very typically the case—then the water supply will have a negligible impact on health. The reason is that only water quality has been changed. Water quality affects only the water-borne component of group 1 and, if that water-borne component is small, there will be little impact on health.

This little story may explain why some studies on the impact of water supplies on health have failed to demonstrate a significant impact and why, in general, rural water programmes

Fig. 2. An unimproved well in Northern Nigeria. Water in such a well will certainly be heavily polluted and may be a significant cause of water-borne infection. In addition, a well of this kind may be an important focus for Guinea worm transmission (Photo: R. G. Feachem).

are not improving community health in the way that governments and donor agencies anticipate. The implications of this state of affairs for future research priorities will now be considered.

WHAT WE KNOW AND WHAT WE DON'T KNOW

We know that good domestic water supplies in every home are a vital part of the wide ranging environmental improvements which, together with wealth, have caused such a dramatic reduction in infectious disease in Europe and North America in the last 100 years.

We know that if it were possible to transform the socio-economic, and environmental conditions (including water supply) of the poor in developing countries into those enjoyed in Europe or North America, a very dramatic reduction in infectious disease would follow.

We know that improvements in environmental conditions must include good water supplies if they are to have their full effect on community health.

We do not fully understand the role of partial and limited improvements in environmental quality as opposed to comprehensive improvements.

Fig. 3. An unprotected water source in Lesotho containing 1000 E. coli per 100 ml. (Photo: R. G. Feachem).

We do not know what is the potential role of water supplies constructed in the absence of other inputs or changes and designed to low-cost specifications.

We suspect that replacing dirty water by clean water in the absence of other inputs, will often have little effect on health.

We know that it is difficult to induce changes in hygiene and water use practices but *we suspect* that such changes may be essential if improved water supplies are to improve health.

We suspect that bringing plentiful water close to, or into, houses and providing washing and laundry facilities may improve health in many cases.

Following from this I will now outline some of the areas on which future research efforts might usefully concentrate. The coverage is by no means total and reflects in part my personal interests and my intuitions concerning which research areas will prove most fruitful.

EVALUATION

Whatever are the interrelationships between water and health, there will clearly be no widespread health benefits unless a country has an efficient and effective rural water programme. It is of particular importance that water supplies, once built, continue to operate and deliver water (Cairncross and Feachem, 1977). Retrospective evaluation of a rural water programme can produce valuable information on how the programme may be improved and also may allow the health impact to be estimated. A methodology for such evaluations has now been prepared (Cairncross *et al.*, 1978).

A major increase in the amount of evaluation work undertaken would be beneficial in promoting improvements in programme planning, policy and execution.

CHILDREN

The diseases we regard as water-related are commonly most prevalent among children. This is especially true of many infections in the fecal-oral group such as diarrheas, dysenteries, cholera and ascariasis. Yet in most studies we investigate the water use and hygienic habits of adults. It is imperative that the water use and hygiene patterns of children be studied in detail and be given greater emphasis than the behaviour of adults.

Briscoe (1977) has drawn attention to this point in relation to the study of tubewells and cholera in Bangladesh. In parts of that country, two different qualities of water will be kept in the house. In one jar will be tubewell water of good microbiological quality but with a high iron content. This will be used for drinking. In the second jar will be surface water, which may well contain pathogens, but which will not have a high iron content. This may be used for washing and cooking. In such a situation it is clearly necessary to know exactly how children use the water in the two jars, since cholera has its highest incidence among children.

A similar argument applies to the study of all aspects of hygiene, excreta disposal and social interaction among children if one is studying the epidemiology of diseases which occur primarily in childhood.

WATER USE PATTERNS

Much of the discussion of water-related disease transmission presented above illustrates the central importance of improving hygiene and changing water use patterns. However, very little is known about what kind of external stimuli will promote a greater use of water and an improvement in personal and domestic hygiene.

Detailed research is required into existing water use patterns and preferences and into the impact on these of improvements in water supply hardware. Such research is currently being conducted in Bangladesh by John Briscoe.

More sophisticated models of water source choice are required in order to be able to predict with confidence who will use a particular new water source and for what purposes they will use it. This is especially important in areas like Bangladesh where multiple water sources are available within a few hundred metres of the home.

There is evidence that the provision of individual house connections will promote a three- or four-fold increase in *per capita* water use. However, we need to know the effect of more limited improvements in water supply and how they may be combined with educational efforts to induce improved hygiene and greater water use. We also need to know much more about how bathing, washing and laundry facilities may be combined with public taps in order to improve hygiene and of the acceptability of these facilities in various cultural settings.

WATER QUALITY

In assessing the role of truly water-borne disease in a particular locality, very detailed information on water quality is required. In some studies samples are taken every few days, or every few weeks, from a variety of sources and this information is said to define the water quality. However, transient, but very substantial variations in water quality occur, especially in surface-water sources and especially during rainfall (Feachem, 1974). Very intensive sampling of selected sources over short periods is therefore required if the microbiological quality of the water being used is to be fully understood.

Substantial pollution, occurring between collection of water at the source and eventual use in the home, has now been documented (Soundy and Rivera, 1972; Feachem *et al.*, 1978). The reasons for this, its epidemiological significance and possible preventive measures require more study. The role of residual chlorine levels at the tap in preventing subsequent contamination in the home should be investigated.

It is necessary to test specifically for fecal bacteria and the use of the total coliform count on unchlorinated water supplies should be rejected. Fecal coliforms and fecal streptococci provide good fecal indicators but more work is required to improve the specificity of available tests and the ease with which these tests may be conducted in the field. Research is also required into methods for distinguishing between human and non-human fecal contamination. This is especially necessary where diseases caused by pathogens which primarily infect man (e.g. cholera and shigellosis) are being investigated. A tentative method proposed by Feachem (1975b) has received limited application (Feachem *et al.*, 1978) but is very far from being a standard method.

INDICES OF HEALTH

Investigations into the health impact of water supplies are often complex , costly and time consuming. This is especially true where water-related morbidity is being surveyed. The development of standard indices of water-related morbidity would greatly assist the rapid study of health impact.

The most promising development in the field has arisen from a suggestion by Jelliffe (1972) that skin diseases are a sensitive index of personal hygiene. Work is now in progress (Porter, 1977) on the development of a dermatological index of hygiene. This index could provide a relative measure of the amount of water-washed diseases transmission occurring in a community and its value could be routinely monitored at little cost during the progress of a water supply programme.

A suitable index of water-borne disease transmission will be much harder to develop.

EPIDEMIOLOGICAL MODELLING

Much work has been done in the last 50 years on the mathematical modelling of some water-related infections—notably malaria and schistosomiasis. Such models are invaluable in understanding the dynamics of a disease and in predicting the effect of a particular intervention.

Some work has also been done on the fecal-oral group of infections—notably on typhoid (Cvjetanovic *et al.*, 1971) and cholera (Uemera *et al.*, 1971). However, these models have been little used in practice and there is insufficient knowledge of some of the basic parameters—especially on infective doses.

More research on the modelling of the major fecal-oral infections might well yield insights and assist our understanding of the role of environmental interventions such as water supplies.

THE CAUSE OF DIARRHEAS

One problem with any investigation of water and health which includes diarrheal disease is that, in many tropical communities, we have little idea what causes diarrhea. One is therefore studying the impact of water on a group of infections of undetermined etiology.

In a recent study in Lesotho, for instance, all diarrheas reported to clinics or a hospital were lumped together and the impact of water upon them was investigated (Feachem *et al.*, 1978). However, there were no data on the etiology of these diarrheas and so the negative findings of this study are difficult to interpret epidemiologically.

This problem does not arise with other water-related infections, such as scabies or ascariasis, where the etiology is clear. In cases where the impact of water supplies on diarrheal disease is being investigated, a thorough study of the etiology of diarrheas in the region will greatly improve our understanding of why a particular water impact is recorded. Current research into viral diarrheas, and the role of *E. coli* in diarrheal disease, may be especially helpful in determining the etiology of hitherto undifferentiated diarrheas.

DIARRHEAL DISEASE SURVEYS

Many previous and on-going studies of the health impact of water supplies have included surveys of diarrheal disease. A common methodology has been to set up a surveillance system in which each household is visited once a week and questioned about episodes of diarrhea occurring in the house since the last interview. Despite the well documented problems of defining "diarrhea", some investigators have hoped that this survey method provides a relatively objective measure of the true incidence of diarrheal episodes in the community.

However, a recent finding in Bangladesh has high-lighted the possible pitfalls inherent in this method. In a survey of two groups of villages (having populations of around 9000 and 7500) over a one year period it was found that, in area A the attack rate from diarrheas and dysenteries was 137/1000/yr, while in area B it was 203/1000/yr (Rahaman *et al.*, 1977). It is believed by the researchers (Rahaman, personal communication) that the areas are essentially homogeneous and that the recorded difference in attack rates is spurious and is caused by gross under-reporting in area A. The explanation for this may be that area B had a hospital, run by the research project, during the period of the survey and this hospital provided quick and effective treatment for persons with acute diarrheal disorders. It is suggested that the villagers in area B were motivated to report accurately their diarrheas because they perceived the benefits of the hospital, while in area A, the lack of treatment facility led to substantial under-reporting.

This finding suggests that the accuracy of reporting in weekly household surveys is highly influenced by other activity in the area and particularly by the subjects' perceptions of the benefits which may accrue to them if they cooperate in the survey. Laboratory confirmation of specific diarrheas does not overcome this problem, because stools or swabs are only collected from individuals who admit to a recent episode of diarrheas. Thus, in the study referred to above, the confirmed rate of shigellosis in area A was 12/1000/yr while, in area B, it was 38/1000/yr. Indeed, laboratory confirmation may make the under-reporting worse because an individual is disinclined to admit to a diarrheal episode if he knows he will then be asked to produce a stool specimen or allow a rectal swab to be taken.

These speculations suggest that it may be preferable to concentrate on regular prevalence surveys of a variety of parasitic infections in which *all* individuals in a given age group are exposed to laboratory examination of feces and blood and also are diagnosed by inspection for infectious skin and eye disease. This may have advantages over trying to determine the true incidence of a group of diarrheal disorders, many of which are mild and many of which are of undefined etiology.

THE QUESTION "WHY?"

It is a recurring feature of the literature on the health impact of water supplies and excreta disposal facilities that an impact, or more usually a lack of impact, is unaccompanied by any satisfactory explanation. Thus, for instance, we may read that cholera is unaffected by tubewell use in Bangladesh (Curlin *et al.*, 1977) but we are not told *why*.

The question "why?" is the most important question. To know that there was not a health impact in a given location is of little help to the policy maker. What he wants to know is how he may change the rural water programme in order to maximize the health benefit and for this it is necessary to know *why* a particular effect was observed.

It follows that an approach to water impact studies which limits itself to the study of morbidity will be inadequate. It is necessary to collect data on the many factors which will help *explain* the effect on morbidity which is recorded. Some of these factors have been referred to in the preceding sections. The role of the social anthropologist, in collecting data on what people actually do, will often be especially valuable in answering the question "why?".

We should not conduct research into the health impact of water supplies in order to know whether to build more water supplies. Water supplies will continue to be built, irrespective of evidence for health benefits, because they fulfil the legitimate political objectives of many governments. We should conduct research in order that water supplies may be built better and may have a greater impact on health.

REFERENCES

Bradley, D. J. and Emurwon, P. Predicting the epidemiological effect of changing water sources, *E. Afr. Med. J.*, **45**, 284-291 (1968).

Briscoe, J. The role of water supply in improving health in poor countries, Paper presented to the US National Academy of Science Workshop on *Effective Interventions to Reduce Infection in Malnourished Populations*, Haiti, June 13-16, (1977).

Cairncross, A. M., Carruthers, I., Curtis, D., Feachem, R. and Bradley, D. J. *Evaluation for Village Water Supply Planning: A Handbook*, manuscript prepared for the WHO International Reference Centre on Community Water Supply, The Hague, (1978).

Cairncross, A. M. and Feachem, R. G. A. Operation and maintenance of rural water supplies, *The Courier*, **43**, 57-59 (1977).

Curlin, G. T., Aziz, K. M. A. and Khan, M. R. The influence of drinking tubewell water on diarrhoea rates in Matlab Thana, Bangladesh, Working Paper No. 1, Cholera Research Laboratory, Dacca, (1977).

Cvjetanovic, B., Grab, B. and Uemera, K. Epidemiological model of typhoid fever and its use in planning and evaluation of antityphoid immunisation and sanitation programmes, *Bull. Wld Hlth Org.*, **45**, 53-75 (1971).

Duguid, J. P., Darekar, M. R. and Wheater, D. W. F. Fimbriae and infectivity in *Salmonella typhimurium*, *J. Med. Microbiol.*, **9**, 459-473 (1976).

Feachem, R. G. A. *Domestic water use in the New Guinea Highlands: the case of the Raiapu Enga*, Water Research Laboratory Report No. 132, University of New South Wales, Sydney, (1973).

Feachem, R. G. A. Faecal coliforms and faecal streptococci in streams in the New Guinea Highlands, *Water Res.*, **8**, 367-374 (1974).

Feachem, R. G. A. Water supplies for low income communities in developing countries, *J. Environ. Engng Div. Am. Soc. civ. Engrs*, **101** (EE5), 687-702 (1975a).

Feachem, R. G. A. An improved role for faecal coliform to faecal streptococci ratios in the differentiation between human and non-human pollution sources, *Water Res.*, **9** (6), 689-690 (1975b).

Feachem, R. G. A. Infectious disease related to water supply and excreta disposal facilities, *Ambio*, **6** (1), 55-58 (1977a).

Feachem, R. G. A. Water supplies for low-income communities: resource allocation, planning and design for a crisis situation, in *Water, Wastes and Health in Hot Climates*, Feachem, R., McGarry, M. and Mara, D. (eds) John Wiley, London, (1977b).

Feachem, R. G. A. Environmental Health Engineering as human ecology: an example from New Guinea, in *Subsistence and Survival*, Bayliss-Smith, T. and Feachem, R. (eds) Academic Press, London, (1977c).

Feachem, R. G. A., Burns, E., Cairncross, A. M., Cronin, A., Cross, R., Curtis, D., Khan, M. K., Lamb, D. and Southall, H. *Water Health and Development: An interdisciplinary evaluation*, Tri-Med Books, London, (1978).

Hollister, A. C., Beck, M. D., Gittelsohn, A. M. and Hemphill, E. C. Influence of water availability on *Shigella* prevalence in children of farm labor families, *Am. J. Publ. Hlth*, **45**, 354-362 (1955).

Hornick, R. B. *et al.* The Broad Street pump revisited: response of volunteers to ingested cholera vibrio, *Bull. N.Y. Acad. Med.*, **47** (10), 1181-1191 (1971).

Levine, R. J., Khan, M. R., D'Souza, S. and Nalin, D. R. Failure of sanitary wells to protect against cholera and other diarrhoeas in Bangladesh, *The Lancet*, **2**, 86-89 (1976).

Jelliffe, D. B. Dermatological markers of environmental hygiene, *The Lancet*, **2**, 49 (1972).

Jordan, P., Woodstock, L., Unrau, G. A. and Cook, J. A. Control of *Schistosoma mansoni* transmission by provision of domestic water supplies, *Bull. Wld Hlth Org.*, **52** (1), 9-20 (1975).

Moore, B. Observations pointing to the conjunctiva as the portal of entry in salmonella infection of guinea pigs, *J. Hyg. Camb.*, **55**, 414 (1957).

Moore, H. A., De La Cruz, E. and Vargas-Mendez, O. Diarrhoeal disease studies in Costa Rica: IV. The influence of sanitation upon the prevalence of intestinal infection and diarrhoeal disease, *Am. J. Epidemiol.*, **82** (2), 162-184 (1965).

Porter, M. J. An epidemiological approach to skin disease in the tropics, *Trop. Doctor*, **7**, 59-66 (1977).

Rahaman, M. M., Aziz, K. M. S., Huq, E. and Rahman, M. M. *Incidence and mortality due to dysentery and diarrhoea in Teknaf—a rural Bangladesh Village: impact of a simple treatment centre*, duplicated report, 8 pp., Cholera Research Laboratory, Dacca, (1977).

Saunders, R. J. and Warford, J. J. *Village Water Supply: Economics and Policy in the Developing World*, John Hopkins Press, Baltimore, (1976).

Soundy, J. and Rivera, H. Acute diarrhoeal disease; Longitudinal study of a sample of the Salvadorian population. II Techniques: Analysis of faeces and food, *Revta Inst. Invest. Med., San Salvador*, **1** (3), 315-316 (1972).

Subrahmanyam, D. V. Community water supply and excreta disposal in the developing countries. *Ambio*, **6** (1), 51-54 (1977).

Uemera, K., Cvjetanovic, B., Sundaresan, T. K., Burua, D., Grab, B. and Wanatabe, Y. *Modèle epidémiologique du choléra: ses applications à la planification des programmes de lutte et l'analyse des coûts et avantages*, WHO/BD/Choléra/1971, World Health Organization, Geneva, (1971).

White, G. F., Bradley, D. J. and White, A. U. *Drawers of Water: Domestic Water Use in East Africa*, University of Chicago Press, Chicago, (1972).

WHO *World Health Statistics Report*, Vol. 26, pp. 720-783 (1973).

WHO *World Health Statistics Report*, Vol. 29, no. 10 (1976).

Technological and Economic Aspects of Water Development

"We don't fly in airplanes which have a 50% failure rate."

David Henry

Water Supply & Management, Vol. 2, pp. 365-372.
© Pergamon Press Ltd., 1978. Printed in Great Britain.

0364-7714/78/0801-0365$02.00/0

Designing for Development: What is Appropriate Technology for Rural Water and Sanitation?

DAVID HENRY

"Weapons determine tactics, tactics do not determine weapons."
Hannibal

If the airplanes in which we travelled to this meeting had the same failure rate as most of the technology that has been applied in the last decade in rural water programmes, 50% of us would not have reached our destination.

In preparing this paper I was forced to make a decision between the two choices: either to describe the technology research and development that IDRC is currently funding, or to give a broader overview of the philosophy and methodology which guide our decision-making. I have opted for the latter, because I think it is more important at this point to describe the "why" and "how" of the process. Before I proceed any further, let me ask you: who carries the water?

One of the most glaring weaknesses in the rural water technology discussion thus far, has been that women have not been encouraged to participate in the dialogue. Women carry almost 100% of the water used for domestic purposes and, in many cases, spend more than 50% of their time doing so. This is a tremendous waste of time, energy and resources. While it may not be possible to put a monetary value on the worth of the time and labour saved when water is made more accessible, one can say with assurance that, until this obstacle is overcome, it will be difficult for rural areas to achieve a significant breakthrough in agricultural production.

The focal point for this discussion is the 90% of the populations of developing countries who live in rural areas. The environments in which they live range from the relatively well-off villager in the Punjab of north India to the hard-pressed villager of Upper Volta. Villagers generally have limited access to the formal power structure, and the poorer they are, the less accessible it is. The power structure can be characterized in two terms: one is political power and the other, energy sources. In traditional societies the *non-conventional energy sources* are the electric motor and the diesel engine. These arrived on the scene in rural areas in developing countries only in the last 2 decades. On the other hand, the *conventional energy sources*, animal and human power, supplemented in a very few cases by wind and water power, have been the mainstays of these societies and economies for centuries.

I am reluctant to describe the research work that has been done thus far as "results". The research can only be described as "results" after the most important components of the research have been completed, that is, the testing of the concept and the technology by the villagers themselves. I would prefer to give you a review of what is happening in the field of low-cost manual pumping technology, wind energy and alternative technologies for excreta disposal at the end of this paper.

However, before I deal with those topics, I want to give you some background to the research philosophy upon which this work is based, and to point out what I consider to be the major obstacles impeding the development and introduction of technologies for traditional societies.

First let me describe IDRC's research philosophy:

1. *National priority*: Any research project should represent an expressed priority for dealing with a concrete problem.

2. *Utilization of local personnel and resources*: The primary responsibility for design and implementation of the project lies with the local researchers.

3. *Rural emphasis*: IDRC gives priority to projects related to the problems of rural or marginal populations who generally have not benefited from technological progress to the same extent as urban people.

4. *Applicability*: The methodology and the results of the proposed research should be widely applicable in the country and in the region where the work is done. (IDRC promotes exchange and dissemination of ideas and experiences among countries and regions of the developing world.)

5. *Research training*: The potential of the project for training and increasing research capability at both the individual and institutional levels is an important element in IDRC projects.

HOW DO WE DEFINE TECHNOLOGY?

The most useful definition of technology for this discussion is: "The totality of the means employed to provide objects necessary for human sustenance and comfort". Although later in this paper I will make specific reference to some particular pieces of machinery, I would like to make it clear that technology to me is a complex blend of social, technical, economic and political forces. In many cases, the technology problems we are facing can be traced back to the very limited perspective that many people have used in defining the term. I would even go so far as to suggest that we must very soon begin to regard our international development institutions as technologies, and we must also begin to ask how appropriate they are.

Having opened the subject of institutional appropriateness, I would like to pose some questions about the institutions which are responsible for allocating resources and delivering technology and expertise in the rural water field. Here one must ask how effective are we in preparing people who are assigned the task of transferring experience and knowledge in the development business. How clearly do we define the nature of the problems we propose to solve?

We must realize that many of the people engaged in planning and implementation of rural water projects in developing countries are products of highly structured and specialized training programmes, designed to produce engineers and technicians whose role is to plan, implement and maintain sophisticated urban water treatment and distribution systems in industrialized countries. This background, when transferred into the extremely different environments in rural areas in developing countries, often leads to the imposition of technology which bears very little relevance to the local situation and cannot, in most cases, be sustained by the local people after the expatriate engineer has departed. It is reasonable to assume that some of these problems could be avoided if the expatriate engineer were able to spend a few weeks at the beginning of his assignment getting to know the people and the country. However, in most cases the engineer is based in the capital city, where his job is to produce plans, and his visits to the rural areas are brief and cursory. A good planner must know the people and if he does not, the plans are often pre-destined to fail. One is reminded of the disastrous "Charge of the Light Brigade", which was ordered by a general who had never seen the terrain where the battle was to be fought.

INSTITUTIONAL ATTITUDES

Many of the programme officers in bilateral and international organizations who are responsible for country programmes admit that there is a great weakness in the planning and field implementation of water projects. However, they are quick to point out that this is a product of the environment in which they work. Programme officers' performance is often judged on the basis of the financial magnitude of projects planned and administered, rather than the quality and the effectiveness of the programmes in the field. Also inherent in the process is a heavy bias towards sophisticated equipment. It is far easier, for instance, to deal with a programme requiring $3.0 million worth of drilling equipment than it is to assist a country to plan and design a water project based on local labour and resources.

One of the limitations within the international and bilateral institutions is the tendency of the general programme managers to take refuge behind the statement: "I am not a technical man". It will become increasingly necessary for the generalist to acquire a much better understanding of the technological implications of the decisions that are being made.

THE FINANCIAL INSTITUTIONS

When it comes to water supply, rural people have the cards stacked against them. Rural people are on the fringes of the formal political power structure, which means that the squeaking urban wheel gets the grease, or in this case the funds for the water. Many rural people do not have a revenue collection system through which payments for both capital and operating costs of rural water supply programmes can be collected. This is a situation which does not appeal very much to lending agencies. In a recent discussion with colleagues from one of the international lending institutions, I was informed that rural populations are generally out of luck when it comes to the question of funding for water supply because they do not produce any revenue. I had to quickly explain that this was not only a naive observation, but also totally wrong. The developing countries are based predominantly on agricultural economies and the economy stands or falls on the production of surplus agricultural products for export. Not only that, but it is the rural areas which feed the cities. In one country a study has been made which argues very persuasively that the villagers are in fact subsidizing major urban water programmes. In view of their attitudes, therefore, one must question whether the international and regional financial institutions are, in fact, appropriate technologies when it comes to dealing with rural water supply.

THE SHAPE OF THE PAST

Looking at the history of the last 20 years in the rural water field, we see that the major impetus for development agency involvement in this field came from severe droughts, first in India in 1967 and subsequently in the Sahel. It has been, in many respects, a knee-jerk response to a crisis situation, resulting in the injection of some very sophisticated capital-intensive equipment and expertise. Apart from personal anecdotal evidence, we have very little information on the success or failure of these programmes. Based on my own observations, however, I would suggest that the return on the investment has been very low. In this context I do not speak of return on investment in purely economic terms, but in response to the basic question: "Are these water systems producing any water?". We could proceed from there to questions such as: "What was the actual cost per thousand litres pumped?" "What percentage of the population was served?" Also: "Will it be possible to extend these types of capital-intensive programmes on a large scale to meet the total needs of a rural population?"

WHAT HAVE WE LEARNED?

Being wrong is a creative part of the learning process, and we have a great deal to learn from the experience of the last two decades. The question is: "Do we have a very effective learning situation?". As things stand at the moment, I would say no. The best information is carefully stored away in confidential files or even more inaccessibly in peoples' memories. What we observe at the present time in the learning process in the rural water field, is another example of the trickle-down theory in practice. Very little useful information has been published and it is unlikely that much more useful information will be generated until there is a declaration of a "freedom of information act" in the rural water field. At the present time, the transfer of information is restricted to what is best described as "the old-boy network", and it is inefficient at that. The time has come for everyone to admit that the last two decades have been largely experimental. Many of the experiments, i.e. projects, have been unsuccessful. If we can all agree that we are in the same leaky boat, we can begin to work out a system for problem-solving.

One of the most essential tools in the rural water field will be an effective system for the generation, collection and dissemination of information. We must, however, be very aware of one fact and that is, information in itself is silent; it is the use to which it is put, in terms of inferring, interpreting, projecting, analysing and decision-making that is important. The development of an effective system for conveying the information to policy-makers and planners who are allocating scarce resources in the water field, is one of the most challenging tasks that faces those of us who are concerned about improving the situation in the field.

SELECTING TECHNOLOGY

Who selected this technology? Let us define the word "select". A useful dictionary definition of the word "select" is: "Exclusively or fastidiously chosen, often with regard to social, economic or cultural characteristics". This question was posed by a colleague, after he heard a description of the technology problems being encountered with conventional manual powered cast-iron pumps in India, where reliable estimates indicated that 80% of the 50,000 wells in drought-prone, hard-rock areas were not producing any water because the pumps had broken down. The only reply I could give was that no-one really selected the technology, but that the technology was grabbed from the inventory of machines most familiar to the engineers in the field.

DESIGNING FOR DEVELOPMENT

Based on our observations of the shape of the past, IDRC has decided that resources must be allocated to solving some of the basic problems in the rural water technology field. Some of the basic criteria for our involvement in this field are: any technology must be capable of fabrication, as far as possible, within the developing country; it must be reliable, have a reasonable cost, and should be maintainable by villagers. This exercise has required the definition of the sets of situations in which the technology would be applied, and the capacities of countries at different levels of development to fabricate these technologies. In many ways, the guiding philosophy for the research is "to seek simplicity and, at the same time, to mistrust it".

Two of the most useful reference works that we use in our research work are *De Re Metallica* by Georgius Agricola, written in 1556, and a book entitled *Technological Forecasting* by Marvin C. Cetron, written in 1969, which is a state-of-the-art review of how the American military establishment forecasts technological requirements for military purposes. This combination of the intuitive and practical knowledge of Mr. Agricola and the precision of military technologists sets a useful stage for allocating resources for technology research for rural communities in developing countries.

Let me try to describe briefly where we stand in the research and development scenario. Figure 1 is an attempt to illustrate the current situation.

In the top left-hand box, we have the research and development establishments in industrialized countries, which are responsible for producing technology for industrialized societies. Industrialized societies are indicated by the box in the lower left.

The industrialized societies produce materials, equipment and expertise, some of which are transferred directly to the modern sector of developing country societies. Some good examples of these technologies are telecommunications, power and transportation.

Some technologies trickle through the modern sector into higher income groups of

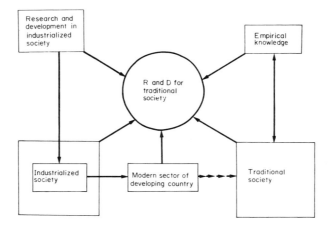

Fig. 1.

traditional societies, which is indicated by the box in the lower right-hand corner. Some examples of these are the transistor radio, the sewing machine and the bicycle.

Traditional societies rely primarily on the empirical knowledge that they have acquired over many centuries. The selection of specific varieties of wood for wheel bearings on bullock carts is a good example.

There is an urgent need to create effective linkages between the institutions and researchers in "orbit" in the centre of the diagram, and the five squares around the perimeter.

It is, therefore, not a matter of designing technology *for* traditional society, but designing technology *in collaboration with* traditional society. Our research funding decisions are influenced very much by a set of questions that were posed by a wise old villager in the State of Rajasthan in India when we were discussing the problem of a broken hand-pump. He said that if a machine was going to be useful to him, it had to be able to stand the test of these three questions: Will it work? Will it last? Can I afford it?

DOWNGRADING TECHNOLOGY

I was introduced to this term by an expatriate technician in Africa recently, who described his work in the "appropriate technology" field as being primarily involved in "downgrading obsolete technology so that it will fit here". I regret very much that my observations in the field indicate that much of what is being described as intermediate or appropriate technology falls into this category. No criteria or objectives are defined for the research, no performance criteria are established for the machines being produced, and no critical evaluation or field testing is carried out.

The frustration that this produces for serious practitioners of rural development is described very well by a man who has been working in rural development in India for the last 30 years. In a recent letter to me, he wrote:

I have been writing at least two dozen letters to various people who are advertising their findings in news-letters like *Wind, Sun and Stars*, but they all seem to have a cozy job they cannot leave, or we cannot find the men who will work in the field and suffer the heat for years. I should like to raise three fundamental questions about the technology research that is presumably being done for developing countries. Firstly, who of these inventors has seen his invention through for at least some years with adequate local spreading results? Secondly, which appropriate technology units are prepared to supply us with a couple of skilful and talented people without demanding heavy salaries and assurances and facilities for personal comfort, etc., to help us set up an operational centre that would help our villages produce, maintain and learn by these technology ideas? Thirdly, where would we find the supporting finance just for basic service machinery and basic food allowances of the people working, at Rupees 250 ($25) per month? If this is not possible, is not all the publicity surrounding the intermediate and appropriate technology somewhat in vain?

What this man is trying to tell us, is that both the machinery and the institutions are inappropriate!

THE APPROPRIATE TECHNOLOGY MARKETPLACE

The most difficult part of the appropriate technology equation is getting the technology into the marketplace after the design has been tested and optimized.

Opinions vary regarding the most effective way to do this. Some people consider that the multinational corporation has very little to contribute to the development of more appropriate technology for developing countries, while others feel that with some encourage-ment, the multinational corporations can make a significant contribution. I belong to the latter. I submit that multinational corporations are amenable to change. They live in the marketplace and can and will respond very quickly to demands in that marketplace. One of the major problems thus far has been that the multinationals have a strong urban bias. We do, however, already have some very useful examples of multinational corporations who have "designed for development" in the rural water field. The two most reliable, and I would say most cost-effective, solutions in the manual pump field have been produced by multinational companies; one is British, the other Swedish. The British company is owned by the American Tobacco Company. The pump it is marketing was invented by a Frenchman in the 1930s and was applied originally in submarines and subsequently in the petroleum and chemical industry. The adaptation was the product of an observation by the international sales engineer who had a very good understanding of the needs of rural communities in Africa. Another low-cost pump design is being developed, based on research which was funded in the early stages by a major plastics manufacturer in Germany. This particular design concept had previously been rejected by a United Nations organization.

Before I am accused of having both feet squarely in the multinational camp, let me stress again that our major emphasis should be to encourage the development of local capacity for technological innovation. However, to dismiss the potential role of the multinationals, which already play a predominant role in the transfer of technology, would be naive and counter-productive.

FINANCING TECHNOLOGY DEVELOPMENT

An OECD publication, *Appropriate Technology Problems and Promises*, published in 1976, states that based on 1975 figures, the amount of money spent worldwide on all research and development for appropriate technology was $5.0 million; compared with $60.0 billion spent on developing new modern technologies for industrialized societies. It is clear that more money must be provided. However, that is only part of the solution. More effective mechanisms for the allocation of this money must be devised if it is going to be accessible to the innovative people in developing countries. One bilateral donor has recently announced a $20 million funding programme for appropriate technology research, but it appears that most of this money will be spent in research institutions and universities in the donor country, with researchers in developing countries getting a trickle from the end of the funding pipeline.

THE SHAPE OF THE FUTURE

I selected Hannibal's quotation for this paper to try to highlight some of the conceptual problems which exist in the rural water technology field. What I observe at the present time is a strong trend among international and bilateral organizations to produce grand strategies for meeting the rural water problems in developing countries. The problem with these grand strategies is that they quite often are based on limited knowledge and experience on the ground. This confusion is compounded by the fact that both the tactics and the weapons for implementing the strategy are inadequate.

We don't fly in airplanes which have a 50% failure rate. Villagers don't want machines which break down and cannot be repaired. The challenge before us is to establish a system which will produce machines that will make poor people more productive—machines that will work, will last, and are affordable. In developing this system, we must ensure that the villager becomes an active member of the research team. For it is the villager, as I said at the beginning, who is the focal point of all this activity, and ultimately it is the villager who will judge if we are making a serious effort to solve his problems, or if we are merely continuing to tinker with his future.

Acknowledgements—I would like to acknowledge the contribution of my colleagues, Dr. Michael McGarry and Tim Journey, many of whose ideas are reflected in this paper. The responsibility for the synthesis, however, is mine.

The views expressed in this paper are those of the author, and do not necessarily reflect the views of the International Development Research Centre.

Water Supply & Management, Vol. 2, pp. 373-386.
© Pergamon Press Ltd., 1978. Printed in Great Britain.

0364-7714/78/0801-0373$02.00/0

Economics of Water Development in Less Developed Countries

L. DOUGLAS JAMES

In 1776, America declared its independence from Great Britain and placed its faith in a philosophy that common people are capable of pursuing and achieving their own best interest without direction from an aristocracy. Also in 1776, Adam Smith published *Wealth of Nations* advancing the philosophy that the economic well-being of common people is better promoted by providing each individual with the freedom to choose in his own best interest than by the most well-meaning choices of a paternalistic despot under the mercantile economic philosphy then prevailing. Separate manifestations of a philosophy of free choice for ordinary people had created a republican government in a new nation with vast underdeveloped water resources and a new science for guiding that development (James and Rogers, 1976).

Over the last 200 years in the United States, the uses made of water for the common good have changed with developing technology and the increase and westward movement of population. Navigation canals opened a rural hinterland to world trade in the early 1800s. Deserts were made productive through irrigation beginning in the late 1800s. Cities were protected from flooding, and hydroelectric power brought energy into homes and revolutionized daily living. Recently, more leisure time has made water-based recreation popular, and a strong environmental concern has made water quality control the primary current resource management goal.

During these same 200 years, the science of economics has developed a systematic methodology for project selection and design. Major contributions were made as Marshall (1890) introduced partial equilibrium analysis as a theoretical base for analyzing government investment alternatives, as Wellington (1887) and Fish (1915) showed how to combine economic theory with engineering data in quantitative project evaluation, as Pareto (1897) and Pigou (1938) formulated the basic theorems used to compare the effects of alternatives on human welfare, as Keynes (1936) provided groundwork for integrating planned budget deficits for public works expansion into an overall macro-economic policy to damp business cycle extremes, and as many recent economists have worked on combining economic with environmental and other goals in multi-objective planning (Cohan and Marks, 1975; Haimes, 1977; Zeleny, 1976).

Water resources planning practice and economic science have developed together in the United States over these last 200 years. Economic principles have provided planners with tools to select better projects, and water resources planning has provided academics with important practical problems for testing their theories. Every application cannot be set forth as an example to be followed: bad projects have been built, and bad theories have been advocated. Nevertheless, the interactive process has produced a set of principles, standards, and procedures designed to guide further water development and manage already developed resources for the common good, the state-of-the-art in 1977 for water resources development in the United States (US Water Resources Council, 1977).

Lesser developed countries should be taking full advantage of this body of theory and practice. Of course, United States practice is not fully applicable; the theory must be reapplied to develop more effective practice in other settings. Surely, water resources professionals can employ their accumulated theory and empirical information in economics, ecology, sociology, political science, etc. to do much better by the currently less developed countries than these sciences did during their developmental stages within the United States over the last 200 years.

OUTLINE OF THE APPROACH

A logical point for beginning discussion on just how the principles, standards, and procedures applied to water resources planning and design should be varied with the degree of economic development and other relevant factors within a country is to review the practices one by one and to determine which developed country practices make sense in a less developed country, which need revision, and what that revision might be. Where the need for change is obvious but the nature of what is needed is not, research can be recommended. Where some change is essential to make reasonable choice on planning issues that must be decided soon, the research should be given high priority.

Naturally it is not possible in one paper to review every facet of water resources planning and accumulate the evidence required to decide what procedures apply in what state of national economic development. What can be done is to review a few major ones. These come in five groups:

1. *Project purposes:* Water projects are constructed for flood control, drainage, water supply, navigation, power, water quality control, recreation, and fish and wildlife control or enhancement. To what extent should the relative emphasis placed on these purposes be varied with the level of a country's development?

2. *Planning objectives*: The federal decision in the United States is to plan water development projects to further economic growth and protect environmental quality while also examining social well-being and regional development factors. Should less developed countries be using different criteria, different weights in evaluating trade-offs among the criteria, or different measurement of a given criterion?

3. *Project level*: Project implementation in the developed countries has passed through the stages of individual non-structural response (e.g. avoiding flood damage by selecting locations safe from flooding), individual structural action (private levees or flood proofing), government structural action (larger levees or reservoirs protecting communities), to governmental non-structural programmes (regulation of flood plain use). The same trend

has occurred in every one of the eight listed project purposes. Should less developed countries move through this same sequence as their water development and management programmes matures, or would a different route be better for them? Should they begin by using modern technology to construct large reservoirs or would they be better advised to concentrate on village wells, small-scale irrigation, and rural sanitation?

4. *Feasibility tests*: Project selection requires testing each alternative according to engineering feasibility (will a given design actually achieve its intended function?), economic feasibility (will the good achieved by the project, be it strictly economic or environmental and social in nature, justify the expenditure to implement it?), financial feasibility (can sufficient funds be obtained to pay the bills?), environmental feasibility (are the environmental changes the project will cause acceptable?), political feasibility (can political approval required for government action be obtained?) and social feasibility (will potential project beneficiaries use the project in the manner and to the degree required for the project to fulfil its intended purpose?). The test for economic feasibility is discussed later in this article. The other tests must also be based on different considerations between developed and less developed countries. The engineering feasibility of a given design depends on local physical, climatic, and geological conditions. Environmental, political, and social feasibility obviously depend on different factors in the setting of a less developed country.

5. *Project design*: Project design requires sequential decision making on location, design dimensions, materials, shape, construction timing, and many others. Each decision would ideally be optimized by choosing the most favourable alternative. However, since such studies are time consuming, many design decisions are not based on separate studies for each application but rather on design standards based on what past practice has shown satisfactory in a particular situation. The important point to remember here is that the satisfying criteria are those of developed countries in western culture. Planners educated in that setting tend to follow these design standards without sufficient consideration of whether they would also result from an optimality analysis based on local conditions. Planners should be asking what differences in type of project design (materials, construction methods, facility selection, etc.) are appropriate for less developed countries, and how should engineering design standards be adjusted to accommodate their needs.

PROJECT PURPOSES

Water projects are constructed either to alleviate some water-related problem such as flooding or pollution, or to realize opportunities to use available resources such as for irrigation or hydroelectric power generation. The importance of pursuing a given purpose to the people of a given country depends on the physical severity of the problem (e.g. depth and frequency of flooding), the number of people affected, and their susceptibility to being harmed (e.g. the use they are making of the flood plain). Each opportunity has an importance that depends on how much additional water is available for development or can be shifted to higher, from lower valued uses and how much benefit will result.

The ideal planning approach would be to explore all water-related problems and opportunities and select those projects (whatever their purpose or combination of purposes) that produce the greatest net benefit. In the real world of political decision making, however, countries have not been able to achieve such balanced resource development (Hirschman, 1958). The United States, for example, has not had a balanced water development programme but has rather gone through successive periods when the major emphasis was placed on navigation, irrigation, flood control, and today water quality control. Water resources development requires a strong and widespread base of political support, and the United States' experience has shown that such public support is not divided equally over the various project purposes.

National priorities need to be decided through the political decision-making process existing within a country. Logically, flood control and drainage would be expected to be more important in wetter climates, water supply in drier climates or more urbanized areas, vector control in tropical climates, and hydroelectric power once a mountainous country has reached a sufficient level of national development to use the energy productively. Recreation and water quality control do not usually gain primary importance until after industrialization. Less developed countries would be best advised to select priority project purposes in order to improve their chances of maintaining the long-term support necessary to accomplish something meaningful. A programme spread too thinly among many purposes is much less likely to be politically viable.

PLANNING OBJECTIVES

Developed countries

The planning objectives on which water projects for a given purpose (and to a lesser extent projects for different purposes are compared) in the United States (US Water Resources Council, 1973) are:

1. Economic efficiency or net benefits to whomsoever they may accrue, translated as best they can into commensurable monetary units. Benefits include direct benefits to users of project output, indirect benefits from technological external effects, secondary benefits from pecuniary external effects, employment benefits through new jobs created or other resources utilized, and land-enhancement benefits through more productive land use. Costs include the one-time costs of implementation, recurring costs of operation and maintenance, and the associated costs required in the private sector to take advantage of the project. Benefits as defined above are more properly called consequences, in that individual items may be either positive or negative. The procedures for estimating benefits in a developed economy, summing them in a cash flow diagram, and discounting the results into a single number for comparative purposes are well developed (James and Lee, 1971).

2. Environmental quality or preserving or enhancing the natural processes which form key links in ecological systems and thereby directly or indirectly contribute to human well-being. Components include contributions through: (a) the natural beauty of open and green space and a wide variety of other scenic areas; (b) archeological, historical, biological, geological, or ecological resources or systems; (c) water, land, and air quality; and (d) protection against the irreversible commitments of resources in manners that might later be regretted. These effects are usually summarized in environmental impact statements tabulating sizes of environmental areas by how they are affected, the quality

of the areas, and the contribution of the areas to human welfare (Black and Herrington, 1974; Corwin *et al.*, 1975). Lists of items to tabulate have been recommended (US Water Resources Council, 1973), but the procedures for collecting the information and interpreting the results are far from standardized. The present goal of environmental impact assessment in the United States is more to identify and publicize the consequences of a proposed action. The procedure has not advanced to the point of being able to use collected factual information to predict how changes in measurable characteristics of the environment would affect either ecological interdependencies or human well-being. No framework is available for aggregating the many dimensions of environmental impact into a single, or even a manageable small group of numbers; no agreement has been reached on how to discount environmental effects at different dates to equivalency at a common date; and we have not even established a consensus on what is an improvement and what is a degradation of the environment.

3. Social well-being or preserving or upgrading the aspects of human well-being that are not quantifiable in terms of income or of characteristics of the natural environment. Whereas the environmental dimensions of well-being are enhanced by approaching a steady balance in the interdependence relationships among ecological systems that is reasonably satisfactory for all involved, the social dimensions are enhanced by approaching a balance in the interdependent relationships among people. The concern is not so much for economic or physical dependencies as on dependencies that are psychological or emotional in nature. The goal of social impact analysis is to predict numbers of people who will find social relationships on which they have grown to depend altered and to classify those counted according to the nature of the dependency, the degree to which it was altered, and the ability of the people affected to withstand the change. The methodology (Finsterbusch and Wolf, 1977; Wolf, 1977) for making these assessments is even less developed than that for environmental impact analysis. Specific information typically considered relevant includes effects on real (i.e. not simply limited to monetary) income; security of life, health, and safety; educational, cultural and recreational opportunities; and preparedness for military and other national emergencies. One useful tabulation is a breakdown of how project benefits and costs divide among people in various income or cultural groups, but even in this example, no ready method exists for associating a given distribution of benefits among these groups to aggregate social well-being. The art has established no consensus for condensing social impact into a relatively simple display for decision makers.

4. Regional development or how economic, environmental, and social impacts vary among the recognized geographical regions (economic trade areas) of a country. The regions to be used are defined, and the impacts in each one are estimated. Here again, the methodology only identifies and publicizes effects as it has not been able to relate the geographical distribution of impacts to the welfare of a country as a whole as is needed to decide whether one distribution or another is to be preferred.

Less developed countries

Obviously, the objectives and the procedures used in evaluating proposed projects with respect to the objectives would not be the same in less developed countries. In fact, each country needs to derive procedures that advance its social welfare function (Bergson, 1966). Definition of the objectives for water resources planning in a less developed country requires a determination of what changes its people would interpret as an improvement in their well-being and of what changes they would find objectionable. Then, before the articulated objectives can be used by planners, practical measurable indicators of progress toward these objectives need to be defined and a theoretical basis and working methodology for predicting how given acts of resource development will alter those indicators needs to be developed.

Social objectives are properly determined through the political process. Idealistically, governments come into, or are forced out of power according to their success in meeting the needs of the population. Practically, no matter how a government came into power, the political leadership of a country has fundamental goals it wants to achieve and programme that it wants to promote. Water resources planners should listen to and as possible interact with (provide information so that the leaders will be better informed) that leadership in defining project objectives.

Experience suggests that first, protection of public health and safety and second, economic development are the primary objectives usually chosen by people who are not well-off economically. Concern for environmental quality tends to increase with affluence (even though the direct effect of environmental change on human welfare is probably greater in more primitive economies). The importance a country places on social goals probably also generally increases with development even though poorer people are more subject to and often less able to cope with the severe effects of abrupt social change. The importance to a country of how benefits and costs are distributed among cultural groups and among geographical regions probably depends mostly on the homogeneity of the population with the least importance being where the country is small and homogeneous and the greatest importance being where the country is closely divided between two rival groups.

Principles and standards for less developed countries

The problems of measuring progress toward selected objectives in less developed countries vary with the objective and how it is defined. Some thoughts on how the procedures outlined above might be varied when applied to less developed countries follow:

1. *Economic efficiency*—(a) Direct economic benefits in developed countries are generally estimated from the value an output would have in a free market under conditions of pure competition or from the cost a free market would charge for producing the same output in an alternative manner (for example, hydroelectric power benefits can be estimated in either manner).

The gross benefit resulting from output marketable under conditions of pure competition, would equal market price times output quantity. However, prevailing market conditions may rob market price of its normative significance through external effects, natural monopoly, outside intervention (price regulation, for example), export-import restrictions, etc. In such cases, shadow prices, estimated by employing a suitable economic model, may be substituted in the calculation. If price or unit value received varies with the amount of project output, the demand curve must be derived so that benefits may be estimated as aggregate value in use (the area under the demand curve over the range of added supply). If no direct market exists for project output, benefits may be imputed from analysis of consequent market gains and losses such as is normally done for irrigation water or flood control (James and Lee, 1971).

Benefit evaluation is much more difficult in less developed countries where national markets are small and greatly affected by major water development projects, the economy is not based on competitive conditions, and data are too limited to estimate how the local economy will be affected. As examples of situations to be overcome, natural monopoly is more likely with smaller markets, export-import considerations become more limiting as more materials have to be obtained from other countries, and market prices are affected more by project output. A large flood can easily be a major blow to a national economy if it destroys key means of production or necessitates repairs temporarily utilizing the capacity of the entire construction industry. Construction of a major irrigation or hydro-electric project may require materials and trained personnel otherwise unavailable in a country and thus necessitate building new plant and implementing new training pro-grammes, possibly leading to severe over capacity within these areas once the project is completed. Irrigation projects may require special training to teach agriculturalists irrigation methods and the development of a new food processing capability and new markets for the produce. Both add to project costs. The materials, trained labour, output purchases, etc. available in developed countries are simply not readily available in most less well developed countries. Some method is needed to evaluate such situations, and the economist must often work from very limited descriptive data on the economy.

(b) Indirect or technological external effects are generally estimated in a developed economy as some fraction (originally estimated through case study evaluations of typical situations) of direct benefits. In less developed countries, the important technological external effects are likely to differ from those important in developed countries and their magnitudes are likely to vary much more from situation to situation but on an average be somewhat smaller (on the assumption that technological linkages will be weaker and fewer). In any event, the percentage used for the estimation of indirect effects in developed countries cannot be assumed applicable in less developed countries.

(c) Secondary or pecuniary external effects in a developed economy were also one largely estimated as percentages, but now input-output modeling (Miernyk, 1966) is gaining increased use. However, in response to strong arguments that secondary effects are essentially zero from the national viewpoint in a large developed economy in times of full employment (Eckstein, 1958), secondary benefits currently play a minor role in water resources planning in the United States. In less developed countries, opposite conditions prevail; and major secondary benefits result from the greater employment of manpower and materials made possible by a project as part of the development process. Furthermore, smaller nations are more likely to experience secondary economic growth as the investment capital comes from outside rather than being diverted from other sectors in the internal economy. In a developed country, secondary benefits are often substantial from a local viewpoint but negligible from a national viewpoint. In less developed countries able to finance water projects from international funding sources, secondary benefits would be substantial even if they were small (not negligible where the economies benefiting have high unemployment rates) from the world viewpoint. The net gain from the international viewpoint is in the social gains of income redistribution toward poorer peoples rather than in greater economic efficiency.

(d) The employment benefits from water resources development are much larger in less developed countries where projects can do a great deal to develop new labour skills, provide work for the unemployed, and enhance labour and resource productivity. Restraining factors include the ability of the country to provide (perhaps beginning from very basic levels) and of the workers to absorb, in the time available, the training required to become employable in more productive occupations. Often, changes in employment imply changes in life style that people are slow to accept. For many less developed countries, resource employment information is limited and procedures for estimating how projects will change employment patterns are poorly developed. Certainly a great deal of research is needed into how water resources development might be more effective in reducing unemployment and underemployment.

(e) One might expect land-enhancement benefits to be generally smaller in countries where relatively more of the land is rural and the economy is less able to absorb the production resulting as new land is developed. In addition, extreme population densities and cultural attitude toward land tenure may substantially reduce flexibility for land use change.

(f) Project costs in less developed countries are likely to be higher overall because material, equipment and specialized labour have to be brought from greater distances. Some costs, however, can often be reduced to the extent that unskilled labour can be profitably substituted for more expensive construction equipment and skilled labour. In the long run, the greater difficulty in keeping a project functional may be with operation and maintenance. Good maintenance requires cooperative interaction (informed complaints) with the people served. Technically qualified people and supporting supplies must be kept for long periods to meet maintenance needs, a task which experience shows to be much more difficult than getting short-term commitments during construction periods. Replacement of machinery or other project elements that wear out may be much more troublesome in countries remote from industrial supplies. Associated costs are likely to be much harder to raise among people of lower income.

2. *Environmental quality*—Each country has its own unique set of scenic, archeological, historical, biological, geological, and ecological resources and systems. Water, land and air quality are more pervasive problems; but here too, a great deal of variation exists in what people want, especially with respect to the aspects that relate to environmental preference than to effects on health or ecology. Consequently, each country needs to develop its own framework for environmental analysis, emphasizing those aspects most important in its setting and to its people and particularly to those people in the immediate vicinity of the project. Multi-objective optimization requires trade-offs in which relatively less value achieved toward one objective is sacrificed to gain relatively more in terms of another objective. Generally speaking, less developed countries will probably be less willing to make economic sacrifice for environmental gain than will the more developed countries whose people are expressing a declining marginal utility of money. In setting its environmental priorities, each nation needs to examine its own resources and the value its people place on them. If environmental impact analysis is ever to progress from the current disputes over what environmental and social effects will result from a given development to scientific evaluations of how water-project-caused environmental change affects ecological and social interdependencies and human well-being, a great deal of research

will be necessary. Only then can debate move from questions of fact to questions of values. Much of the necessary work can be done in the setting of less developed countries because of the unique environmental settings and cultural values they contain. As results become definitive, a significant re-ordering of environmental priorities in the less developed countries may be expected.

3. *Social well-being*—Each country has its own unique social, natural, and physical environments. Consequently, each country also needs its own framework for establishing social effects and relating them to its own values. Less developed countries and particularly their rural people typically have much greater differences between real and monetary income, making it more important for project planners to quantify effects on real income. Often the data available for income determinations is very fragmentary. Less developed countries may be forced by financial constraints into taking greater risks with the health and safety of their citizens. They may place less emphasis than do the more highly developed countries, on recreational opportunities but often place very high priority on preserving important aspects of their cultural heritage. Unstable political situations in or among the less developed countries often makes military preparedness of high priority.

As was emphasized above for environmental quality, considerable research will be needed for more scientific prediction of how water-project-caused social change affects human well-being and how such effects vary with social conditions. Considerable research is also needed to make better predictions of what water-project-caused social changes will likely occur.

4. *Regional development*—Many less developed countries are plagued with vast discrepancies in economic conditions between rapidly expanding economies around the capital city or in more industrialized areas and static backward conditions in rural or more remote areas. People are consequently crowding into large cities and often creating very undesirable highly-congested urban environments. Consequently, water resources development in the areas lagging economically provides some potential for spreading economic growth more widely over a country. Any such project, however, needs to be structured carefully to prevent benefits from concentrating unduly among the few while most of the local people go unhelped.

LEVELS OF ANALYSIS

Most of the effort in water resources development and management actually occurs at the level of the individual. Farmers, villagers, craftsmen, and others in the private sector regularly haul water, develop small irrigation systems, repair flood damage, drain fields, drill wells, dispose of waste materials, etc. at considerable expense to themselves. Many functioning water systems are very primitive and hence tend to be scorned by modern planners (often particularly so by planners who, because they are from the less developed country, tend to be embarrassed by the backwardness of their own people), but it is a mistake in any country to plan water resources development without due consideration of the wants, needs and capabilities of the individuals served (White, 1972). These individuals spend a great deal of their own time and have a strong personal commitment to making sure that their work achieves its intended purpose. This kind of commitment for success tends to be missing in public projects. A project creating incentives that makes these users feel that their own best interest is best served by using project output and making sure that the project continues to function successfully will be many times more successful than one where the users feel better off continuing in their old way or feel uncomfortable with some strange new technology. For example, villagers provided with a new water supply or sanitary system need to be made to feel so much better off with the new technology that they are willing to learn how to take proper care of it when it is working and repair it when it fails.

Water project construction in the United States has moved over the years from small projects implemented and maintained by local users or beneficiaries to much larger projects implemented and maintained by the federal government. The trend has been justified (with good reason) by arguments that the larger projects are so complex technically, so functionally interrelated in the total river system, and financially so expensive that only the federal government has the resources needed to provide the necessary expertise, coordination, and finances. One of the consequences of this trend, however, has been that people who have been able to obtain federally-subsidized flood protection, water supplies, hydroelectric power, sanitation systems, etc. at little cost to themselves, then organized and became a strong political force to keep the benefits coming (Haveman, 1965). The political pressures exerted by these beneficiaries increased project expenditures to more than the people of the country as a whole were willing to pay. In reaction, government is now turning from project construction to non-structural programmes to reduce the need for additional construction through flood plain management, water and energy use restrictions, waste effluent standards, etc.

The same logic used to move water resources development from a local to a national responsibility in the United States in moving water resources development in less developed countries in the direction of more of the expertise and financing coming from international sources. The trend can create a number of problems. Experts from developed countries tend to design projects based on engineering standards, using construction methods, and to meet needs with which they are familiar and which may not be appropriate for less developed countries. The projects may not provide an efficient transition from past, and often very primitive, water management practice. The people may not understand how properly to use, let alone maintain, their new facilities. The result of outside assistance intended to help people toward developed economic independence may, in fact, be making them more dependent on their benefactors for technical and financial aid. The resulting financial drain may well become so unacceptable that international funding sources will either withdraw their support and leave the beneficiary nation to get along as best it can or begin to place restrictions on project management. Either eventuality could have strong adverse consequences on the international scene. Certainly, less developed countries should do their best to formulate water development projects that will lead to greater independence from, rather than greater reliance on, outside aid. Certainly, each less developed country needs to consider both construction projects and non-structural measures from the beginning so that it will not later suffer the adverse consequences of an unbalanced water resource development programme. Certainly, each country needs to be careful in selecting a balance between large river development schemes and local water supply and sanitation projects, between sophisticated capital intensive technology and functional systems understandable by those using them.

FEASIBLITY TESTS

The same series of feasibility tests apply to countries in all states of development, but the appropriate methodology for conducting the tests may vary considerably. Engineering feasibility is affected by differences in climate, local physical conditions, availability of materials and labour, or degree of quality control in construction. Economic feasibility is affected by all the factors affecting benefits and costs.

Financial feasibility may turn out different because the considerations that lead to favourable receptions to projects in a national legislature may not be the same as those that lead to favourable receptions from international funding sources. In less developed countries, loans may be harder to obtain, interest rates paid on borrowed capital may be higher, and the repayment capacity of the beneficiaries may be less. All of these factors favour a less capital intensive technology.

Environmental feasibility may turn out different because of differences in ecological interdependencies (for example between temperate and tropical climates) and differences in ways people view the environment. People in less developed countries may be willing to make greater environmental sacrifices (particularly those that won't affect them for some time) for immediate economic gain than they would later when looking back.

Political feasibility may turn out different because of differences in the political decision-making systems among countries, differences in the values of those in key decision-making roles, and differences in legal constraints on decision-maker prerogatives. Most governments have good political reasons for excluding certain alternatives from consideration.

Social feasibility is likely to be the test that differs most drastically among countries. Project beneficiaries differ greatly in ability or desire to absorb innovation imposed from the outside and in the kinds of innovation that they are willing to accept. One of the greatest challenges in water resources planning, particularly in less developed countries, is to determine how to predict in advance what the public will accept and what it will not. In reality, most changes are increasingly accepted over time and the rate of acceptance may depend more on how the innovations are presented and followed up than on their content. Research that could develop ways to motivate people to use their water (dispose of their wastes) wisely and take advantage of their resources would be very valuable, particularly when physical and financial constraints require greater emphasis on non-structural measures.

PROJECT DESIGN

The three classic questions asked of engineering economy studies are: why do it at all? why do it now? and why do it this way? The sections above relate to the first two questions. This section relates to the third: what is the best design for a given project?

Design optimization requires selection of the most desirable degree of project development and of the least costly (or most desirable in view of multiple objectives) physical design for doing the job. As an example, for flood control, the degree of project development may be indicated by the return period of the design flood. The more infrequent (larger) the design flood, the more the project costs and the more benefit it provides.

Total cost and total benefit may both be plotted against design return period. Total cost normally rises more slowly with project size at first and then more rapidly for larger projects, whereas total benefit normally rises more rapidly at first and then more slowly according to the principle of diminishing marginal return. At some intermediate point, benefits minus cost is maximum and project size is optimum (James and Lee, 1971). Given that project size (e.g. a design to prevent flood damages from the 100-year flood), one can then run a series of engineering economy studies to answer such questions as: what is the optimum combination of reservoir storage and channelization? what is the optimum reservoir site? how should the dam be positioned at a given reservoir site? what size of spillway is needed (in a trade-off between dam height and spillway width)? and what materials should be used in dam construction?

The principle of resolving each question by comparing the alternatives and finding which one maximizes net benefits or minimizes the cost of accomplishing a given task (Grant and Ireson, 1970), is the same for all countries, but one needs to watch a number of subtleties in its application. It is very expensive to make a thorough economic analysis of repetitive design decisions. Many designers develop over the years a "feel" for good design based on their past experience. When asked to design for a less developed country, they may unthinkingly transfer design decisions or construction practices that are unnecessarily costly. Generally speaking, optimal designs for less developed countries will be less capital and more labour intensive, will make greater use of locally available materials, will require greater assistance in training project beneficiaries, and will provide a lesser degree of development than one would expect in more advanced economies.

PRIORITY RESEARCH NEEDS

A great deal can, and should, be done to upgrade the quality of the feasibility studies made in planning water development programmes in less developed countries. The goal of such efforts should be to enhance the usefulness of the studies and the use made of them by decision makers in the respective countries. Sometimes, an experienced planner can readily recommend ways to improve the studies he reviews to increase their usefulness, and at other times research is needed to resolve uncertainty. Each country will find that it will have its own set of priority research items addressing problems impeding its water development programme. The priority given an item on the international scale should logically depend on the number of countries with the problem, the severity of the problem, and the inability of the countries with the problem to deal with it internally. The process of defining such priorities naturally requires inputs from many lands.

Some tasks that are particularly likely to prove important include:

1. Development through interaction between a nation's political leadership and expert water resources planners and related professionals of a viable set of water planning objectives for a country. Political leaders may not be entirely aware of the technical, economic, and social constraints on water resources development while international experts and other professionals are less aware of local conditions and viewpoints. Each country needs to thoughtfully work out its own water development and management priorities. The research objective would be to develop a methodology that countries could use to develop a framework of principles and standards for water resources planning

purposes. Systematic collection of up-to-date information on the priorities currently being employed in various countries would also be very useful.

2. Standardization of procedures such as that for determining shadow prices for estimating economic value for economic feasibility studies. The United States government found it necessary to require federal agencies to use common evaluation methods in order to compare project merits properly, and the international funding agencies need the same kind of uniformity. The practices, however, need to be reliable as well as uniform; and a great deal of research will be needed to develop truly reliable practices for quantifying such effects as real incomes, employment gains, distribution of total benefits among beneficiary groups, etc.

3. Exploration of technological and pecuniary external effects in situations common to less developed countries for the purpose of developing better procedures for estimating indirect and secondary benefits. Particular attention needs to be given to the constraints imposed by limitations in available data and how to make the best possible estimates in spite of such limitations. Important topics of this sort include prediction of how water resources development affects market structure in less developed economies for the purpose of more reliable secondary benefit estimation; analysis of how secondary effects vary with project purpose, design, and operation; and definition of technological external effects commonly found between water resources and other public sector planning in less developed countries.

4. Definition of the ecological impacts of water resources development in tropical settings (both humid and arid) and of the social impacts in the cultures common to the less developed lands. Both types of impacts should be measured in a way that can be related as much as possible to the well-being of the people. Study topics in the ecological and social impact areas include definition of the state of health of a community in a way in which planners can relate health to project design, definition of land quality indicators based on how people are affected and that planners can use to upgrade the quality of life in less developed countries, definition of ecological interdependencies and how they relate to human well-being in tropical conditions, and development of less traumatic methods for resettling rural people and communities displaced by project construction.

5. Exploration of a proper mix of non-structural and structural, individual and group water management programmes for a given setting so that a country will, in fact, become more self-sufficient economically through water resources development. Such studies should define and explore the alternatives for training people how to do such things as make the best use or irrigation and drainage facilities or community water supply and sanitation systems, to respond efficiently to flood warnings, and to recognize the effects of their actions on water quality and downstream water users. Too often the dynamics of achieving efficient project utilization are overlooked by planners thinking only of some eventual, idealized, steady-state condition.

CONCLUSION

The state-of-the-art as developed for water resources planning and management in the United States and the other developed countries has evolved a set of basic principles equally applicable to countries in all stages of economic development. It is very important, however, to emphasize that it is these basic principles and not the results of their application (the standards and procedures specified by the US Water Resources Council) that are the same. The basic principles need to be applied to a great variety of water planning problems in the less developed countries in order to develop a larger body of operating planning tools useful to all nations. Some priority tool-forming studies are recommended in the preceding section. As the research progresses, additional needs will come into clearer focus.

REFERENCES

Bergson, A. *Essays in Normative Economics*, Harvard University Press, Cambridge, (1966).

Black, P. E. and Herrington, L. P. *Working with NEPA: Environmental Impact Analysis for the Resource Manager*, MSS Information Corporation, New York, (1974).

Cohan, J. L. and Marks, D. H. A review and evaluation of multi-objective programming techniques, *Water Resour. Res.*, **11**, 208-220 (1975).

Corwin, R. *et al. Environmental Impact Assessment*, Freeman-Cooper, San Francisco, (1975).

Eckstein, O. *Water Resources Development: The Economics of Project Evaluation*, Harvard University Press, Cambridge, (1958).

Finsterbusch, K. and Wolf, C. P. (eds) *Methodology of Social Impact Assessment*, Dowden, Hutchinson & Ross, Stroudsburg, (1977).

Fish, J. C. L. *Engineering Economics: First Principles*, McGraw-Hill, New York, (1915).

Grant, E. L. and Ireson, W. G. *Principles of Engineering Economy*, Ronald Press, New York, (1970).

Haimes, Y. Y. *Hierarchial Analysis of Water Resources Systems*, McGraw-Hill, New York, (1977).

Haveman, R. H. *Water Resources Investment and the Public Interest*, Vanderbilt University Press, Nashville, (1965).

Hirschman, A. O. *The Strategy of Economic Development*, Yale University Press, New Haven, (1958).

James, L. D. and Lee, R. R. *Economics of Water Resources Planning*, McGraw-Hill, New York, (1971).

James, L. D. and Rogers, J. R. Economics and water resources planning in America: 1876-1976, in *Water Resources Planning in America 1776-1976*, ASCE Preprint 2754, American Society of Civil Engineers, New York, (1976).

Keynes, J. M. *The General Theory of Employment, Interest, and Money*, Harcourt and Brace, New York, (1936).

Marshall, A. *Principles of Economics,* MacMillan, London, (1890).

Miernyk, W. H. *The Elements of Input-Output Analysis*, Random House, New York, (1966).

Pareto, V. *Cours de Economique Politique*, F. Rouge Librarire, Lausanne, (1897).

Pigou, A. C. *The Economics of Welfare*, MacMillan, London, (1938).

Smith, A. *Inquiry into the Nature and Causes of the Wealth of Nations*, London, (1776).

US Water Resources Council, Principles and standards for planning water and related land resources, *Fed. Regist.*, **38**, 24797-24808 (1973).

Wellington, A. M. *The Economic Theory of the Location of Railways*, John Wiley, New York, (1887).

White, G. F. *et al. Drawers of Water: Domestic Water Use in East Africa*, University of Chicago Press, Chicago, (1972).

Wolf, C. P. Social impact assessment: the state of the art updated, *Social Impact Assessment*, **20**, CUNY Graduate Center, New York.

Zeleny, M. *Kyoto 1975*, Springer-Verlag, New York, (1975).

Research Priorities in Water Development

"Is it sometimes or even generally true that research priorities are generated less by the situation of rural people than by preoccupations of professionals?"

Robert Chambers

Water Supply & Management, Vol. 2, pp. 389-398.
© Pergamon Press Ltd., 1978. Printed in Great Britain.

0364-7714/78/0801-0389$02.00

Identifying Research Priorities in Water Development

ROBERT CHAMBERS

This paper speculates on factors influencing priorities in water-related research, suggests complementary and corrective approaches, and presents examples of the sort of priorities which might emerge from using them. The values underlying judgements in the paper concern improving the levels of living of the people, especially the poorer people, in rural areas of the third world. Throughout, "research" includes Research and Development (R and D), and the "natural sciences" are the physical and biological sciences.

The justification for thinking about priorities in water-related research lies paradoxically but precisely in the complexities and difficulties of water as a focus. Its ubiquity in the biosphere and its critical part in photosynthesis and in plant and animal life; its elusive nature, changing so often from one form or medium or combination to another, making it hard to keep track of and measure; the many sources from which it is obtained by man, including condensation, rainfall, springs, rivers, pools, dams and wells; the great number and variety of techniques which are used for allocating, appropriating, transporting and storing it; its many uses by man including drinking, washing, cooking, cooling, watering animals, irrigation and recreation; its seasonal but variable supply to, and removal from, rural environments through tropical weather, setting the patterns of cycles of work and leisure, of health and sickness, of abundance and austerity, of festivals and fasting— these make it as important as it is difficult to encompass in a balanced view.

It is no surprise, then, to find many disciplines engaged on water-related research, including climatology, geology, hydrology, soil science, geography, engineering, agronomy, botany, zoology, medicine, sociology, social anthropology, economics, and most recently political economy, to name but some of those that are prominent in the tropical rural context. With so many specialized points of entry, the danger is that no one will take a balanced view because no one is competent to do so. In these circumstances, multi-disciplinary approaches are called for, but may be merely assemblies of narrow searchlights which illuminate some faces of the subject but leave others in the darkness. Interdisci-plinary research may similarly involve the exchange of insights and methods between disciplines, but may still leave gaps between them. The solution, it will be argued, lies in a different approach to identifying concerns and priorities and in a bold readiness to explore gaps.

AN AGENDA FOR INTROSPECTION

What factors determine priorities, is a question for empirical research. There is no intention in what follows to denigrate good work in the great range of water-related research which has been undertaken, and which, in any case, the writer cannot hope to know about. But in trying to improve decision making about priorities, one must ask whether there are influences—conscious or unconscious—which bend research choices and designs away from what on a stricter and broader view would be high priorities. The points which follow are less assertions of fact than an agenda for introspection for those concerned. They are:

professional training and prestige;
biases of dominance;
difficulties of studying water; and
a problem-orientation.

First, to what extent are research priorities influenced by the skills and concerns of the professions and disciplines available? Hydrologists concern themselves with, for example, the water cycle and the movement of water from one form or location to another. Engineers concentrate on the design and construction of works, using their mathematical skills to calculate stresses, capacities, flows and the like. Soil scientists may try to measure percolation rates in different soils with different water applications. Agronomists investigate crop water requirements. Sociologists study the micro-level village community, the allocation and appropriation of water, the origins and resolution of conflicts. Economists try to calculate the costs and benefits of alternative ways of obtaining or using water, and argue about pricing policies. Medical men estimate levels of pollution, contamination and infection. Each profession and each discipline is pointed towards certain aspects of water such as these, and is programmed with relevant research skills. Moreover, professional prestige and advancement are achieved through work which is highly regarded by fellow professionals. Research tends to use conventional methods and, in Thomas Kuhn's terms (Kuhn, 1962) to be designed to refine existing paradigms. Is it sometimes, or even generally, true that research priorities are generated less by the situation of rural people than by the preoccupations of professionals?

Second, and closely linked, are research priorities subject to biases of dominance, reflecting flows from cores to peripheries: from North to South, from temperate to tropical, from industrial to agricultural, from urban to rural, from research station to its surrounds, from scientist to the (rural, human) objects of scientific investigation? Such flows have in common a top-down, centre-outwards, elitist character. Wisdom, skill and power reside in the centre and are deployed outwards. The political dimensions need no elaboration but the technical aspects are also significant. The disciplines themselves have evolved and become differentiated for other priorities in other environments. The application of disciplines evolved in temperate, rich, industrialized countries may leave gaps or may in other ways be inappropriate in a tropical, poor, rural country. An example of a gap is the management of irrigation bureaucracies, a key subject neglected partly because it was the province of no easily available temperate climate expertise. An example of inappropriateness is the treatment of land and water in agricultural economics. Temperate agricultural economics without irrigation can treat land as a proxy for water since there is a linear relation between the two: land is water-augmenting since water comes from the atmosphere.

In tropical countries the position is often reversed: water, through irrigation, is land-augmenting. It can be asked whether the biases of temperate agricultural economics diffused through professional dominance have not nurtured a tendency, even where water is scarcer than land, to think of yield per unit of land rather than per unit of water, diverting research from critical questions.

Third, are priorities partly determined by the nature of water itself? Not only does it combine with, and separate from, many other inorganic and organic compounds, but in its uncombined forms it flows, seeps and percolates, evaporates, freezes, thaws, condenses and transpires. The weather brings it rather unpredictably into rural environments and then takes it out again. So difficult is it for scientists to measure that they are driven to sharpening the focus of research to make their work manageable and their findings precise. Their searchlights, as it were, narrow their beams to shed a more intense light on a smaller area. As prudent researchers they study the studiable, not only for their PhDs but also during their subsequent professional lives. They may not even try to measure some of the water transferences which, though important, are especially significant (of which the evapo-transpiration from water plants and the water around them may be an example). The problems posed by water as an object of study may, indeed, serve to draw the disciplines apart from one another, or together into rather tight clusters. May the outcome be a sort of micro-myopia, an obsession with one small scene to the neglect of its surroundings?

Fourth, are research priorities influenced by a problem orientation and the selective manner in which problems are perceived? The more obvious problems posed by water include health hazards, floods, droughts, erosion, pollution, silting, and declining water tables. These are all negative aspects of water, problems which with time may become more acute, acquire a political dimension, and generate a demand for research. Such research may, of course, be fully justified. The point is, however, that it is reactive; it is responding to problems that are either visible or political or both. The research is then intended to some extent to identify correcting mechanisms, to contain or overcome the problem or to restore the status quo ante. Research resources may be well employed on such tasks, but they are also preempted from alternative uses. Can a problem orientation, in this sense, have high indirect costs through preventing an opportunity orientation with a more positive approach of seeking to increase the productivity or usefulness of water?

These four linked factors—professional training and prestige, biases of dominance, the difficulties of water-related research, and a reactive problem orientation—might be extended by adding others. Enough should have been said, however, to provoke the reader who is concerned with water-related research to ask self-critically what factors determine priorities and whether those priorities, from the point of view of the rural people, especially the poorer rural people, are suboptimal. Are the values on which "good" research is judged derived from rural needs or from professional training? from the peripheral rural reality or from the dominant norms and ways of thought of the elitist core? from the place of water in the lives of rural people or from the problems of researching and measuring it? from the opportunities for improving the use of water or from the problems which it creates? To what extent is "good" research thought to be research which is methodologically sound, designed to refine a paradigm, related to earlier respectable research, requiring sophisticated equipment and measurement, and enabling the researcher to enhance his reputation with a tidy, citable, footnoted paper with tabulations to two places of decimals, published in a hard international journal? Which, in short, determines priorities more— the rural situation and the needs and wishes of rural people, or the professional situation and the needs of wishes or professionals?

TOWARDS A BALANCED DETERMINATION OF PRIORITIES

Priorities are related to values. If the values stated at the outset of this paper are accepted, then there may be a case for a balancing reversal of flows in determining research priorities, namely: that they should follow not from the urban, rich country, Northern inclinations and perceptions of a professional elite but from the interests of poor rural people; that the prime criterion for good research should be that it is likely to mitigate poverty and hardship among rural people, especially the poorer rural people, and to enhance the quality of their lives in ways which they will welcome; that, in short, priorities should be arrived at less by an overview than by an underview, grounded in the reality of the rural situation. Starting with rural people, their world view, their problems and their opportunities, will give a different perspective. To be able to capture that perspective requires a revolution in professional values and in working styles; it requires that scientists should learn the skills and approaches of anthropologists; it requires humility and a readiness to innovate which may not come easily in many research establishments. The approach at first must necessarily be experimental, involving research and development on Research and Development.

In determining research priorities, more specific criteria are also needed. Some of these will be elicited from the rural people themselves, and will vary from place to place. Others are a matter of personal choice. One short list is:

1. *Productivity*: Insofar as water is scarce, research should pay attention to its sparing use and productivity.

2. *Equity*: Research should be directed to making access to water more, rather than less, egalitarian, and using it to diminish inequalities between individuals and between families.

3. *Stability*: Research should be directed towards achieving stable and renewable water supplies.

4. *Quality of life*: Research should be directed towards enhancing the quality of life of rural people in ways which they welcome. These may include the generation of livelihoods for the poorer rural people, the alleviation of drudgery, the elimination of food shortages and the reduction of disease.

5. *Non-seasonality*: Less obviously, water in tropical climates (much more than in temperate) is a determinant of seasons. Much poverty is reinforced by seasonality; shortages of food and sickness during cultivation limit the crops grown; crops go in distress sales at harvest when prices are low in order to pay off debts; and the next season's cultivation is again limited by shortages of food and by sickness. Water may often be a key to reducing the worst effects of seasonality and helping people to escape from this particular poverty trap.

AN APPROACH THROUGH R AND D ON R AND D

The approach suggested to counterbalance current biases has five main complementary elements:

1. *Working with and learning from rural people*

Rural people know what their life is like and what they do. They know when water is available from what sources. They know how they transport it, how they repair their receptacles, how they manage their irrigation, and how they use water domestically. They know the problems they experience and where it hurts. The housewife in her hut or the farmer in his field may lack specialized technical knowledge but their non-disciplinary underview is more balanced in the range of its insights then the disciplinary overview of the visiting scientist. A first step, then, is to learn how to learn from rural people. A second step is to understand their daily life and needs and to identify problems and opportunities. And a third step is, with them, to develop ways of overcoming those problems and exploiting those opportunities.

2. *Holistic appraisal*

The entire rural environment, including its micro-environments, is potentially relevant. What has been called a "Gandhian-Systems Approach" (Chaturvedi, 1976, p. 75) can be developed to combine the holism of the villagers with the technical insights of outsiders. Care is needed to follow water through its flows, allocations, appropriations, transformations and uses, including stages and aspects which do not fall neatly into the lap of any specialist. The linkages between the physical aspects and the human behavioural aspects may need special attention.

3. *Opportunity orientation*

A reactive problem orientation—dealing with bilharzia, floods, salinity, drought and the like—is useful but should be balanced by a positive opportunity orientation which sees water as a resource capable of multiple exploitations in conjunction with other resources.

4. *Creative lateral thinking*

Because much research is cramped by disciplinary rigour, the scope for creative lateral thinking may be extensive. In identifying research priorities in any field, there is a stage for encouraging flights of imagination to generate new ideas, a few of which may turn out to be very useful. To pursue this approach needs innovation in the social psychology of research. In particular natural scientists and social scientists have much to gain by questioning one another and learning from one another how to see familiar questions from new angles. This suggests free interaction between disciplines and the exchange of insights, ways of thought and modes of analysis. It requires that those taking part should be open and undefended; for it may be only by becoming vulnerable to one another that a group of people can be optimally inventive.

5. *Practicality*

It is not enough for research to establish new knowledge. That new knowledge has to be applied. It is here that both natural and social scientists so commonly and so disastrously fail. Adept at analysis and criticism, they are inept at making the leaps from understanding to prescription and from prescription to implementation. One corrective is a much closer involvement in longer-term action research with opportunities for iterative feedbacks between programme experience and analytical research. Another is that professionals involved with rural water should themselves take part in implementation.

AN ILLUSTRATIVE GAP: IRRIGATION MANAGEMENT IN SRI LANKA

Some of these points can be illustrated from an example in the field of irrigation (for more detail see Chambers, 1975, pp. 2-5).

Large-scale irrigation systems have attracted much attention. Proposals for new systems are subjected to intensive investigation by teams of high-powered experts. The assumption has been, it seems, that if a team was sufficiently multi-disciplinary, all relevant aspects would be covered. In the case of the Mahaweli Ganga project in Sri Lanka, the largest irrigation project in the island, many international experts were mustered to investigate, scrutinize and develop proposals. Each did what he knew how to do. They concluded that although 1.5 million acres were potentially irrigable, only 900,000 acres could be irrigated because of shortage of water. This being so, a critical issue in their appraisal, it might be supposed, would have been the organization and operation of the bureaucracy which was to control and issue the water. It was already well known in Sri Lanka that permissive issues of water by irrigation staff (notably on the Gal Oya project) were a major factor limiting the acreage irrigated. The multi-disciplinary team was, further, explicitly enjoined to examine organizational and management problems in existing irrigation and settlement schemes. In the event, however, there is little in the three volumes of their main report that has any bearing on the organization and operation of the proposed irrigation system. Although the third volume is entitled "Organisational and Management Requirements", the main presentation on irrigation management is less than a page and is concerned with organizational structure and not with operating arrangements, compared with an average of eight pages each for four other subjects: the supply of agricultural inputs; marketing; agricultural credit and cooperatives; and agricultural research, extension and education. What might have been considered the most central question of all is almost completely ignored.

For our purposes it is revealing to look at the report of the sociologist (Barnabas, 1967). As might be expected, he conducted surveys: one of people in irrigation colonization schemes; and one of colonization officers. At least three of his survey findings pointed straight at lower level water management as a concern. For example, when people were asked "what more do you want the administration to do for you?" a majority mentioned better irrigation facilities; and in reporting this he comments: "It seems that the functions of the Irrigation Department need to be looked into in the Colonies". But at the end of his report there are 23 recommendations, none of which mentions water. In this example, the sociologist, starting by learning from the local people, was pointed straight at a key central problem but neither he nor any of his colleagues were able or willing to follow up the pointer.

The lessons are useful. Making a team multi-disciplinary does not necessarily mean that all relevant aspects will be covered. The most significant aspects may not be in the domain of any available discipline, as in this case. Nor will calling the research "inter-disciplinary" necessarily help. Inter-disciplinarity can mean collaboration and exchange of ideas and methods between disciplines. It by no means ensures a holistic view of an environment, and may also leave gaps. In contrast, asking the rural people in this case did point to a gap—the organization and management of irrigation control staff—which presented a major problem and opportunity but which the multi-disciplinary team did not tackle.

The management of those who operate canal irrigation systems has since become a subject for research, notably in the pioneering work of Bottrall (1975) and Wade (1975, 1976a, 1976b). For the future, a body of knowledge and an expertise should gradually be developing for use on appraisal teams and consultancy. That it does not already appear to exist is a dramatic illustration of the inappropriate conservatism of core-periphery disciplinary flows. Work in such a no man's land does not in the short run bring conventional professional rewards; but in the long run its contribution to development and to the poorer rural people may be out of all proportion to the numbers of people who undertake it. What is difficult to understand is the blindness and lack of imagination which failed earlier to identify this gap and to encourage and sponsor research on it. Finally, this example raises the wider question of what other gaps there may be for similar reasons in other water-related fields.

SOME PRIORITIES FOR RESEARCH

It may be rash, having argued that priorities should be generated from a holistic view of particular environments, to suggest priorities which may have more general application. Each reader will have his own ideas arising from his own experience and imagination and the environments which he knows. Suffice it here to list some of the fields where changes following on from water-related research might help rural development generally and the poorer rural people in particular. There are, of course, many other priorities. The point of mentioning these is that they follow on from the argument and may not receive the attention or resources they deserve.

Water reform

The potential for increased agricultural production and more equitable distribution of water to farmers on existing medium and large irrigation systems is probably enormous, not least because production potential has been greatly enhanced by the new agricultural technologies of the past decade. But, as already seen for Sri Lanka, performance on most irrigation systems is very inefficient and falls far below expectations. In Pakistan, for example, it has been calculated that the improved management on existing irrigation could save more than three times the water that will be supplied by the Tarbela dam (costing $1.2 billion). More generally, the supply of water is frequently inequitable, with those at the head receiving more than their fair share, and those at the tail receiving amounts which are small, uncertain, and untimely, if indeed they receive any water at all.

Diagnosis tends to be inadequate because of disciplinary blinkers. Engineers are concerned with physical works and water flows, agronomists with crop water requirements, sociologists with organization and access within communities, and economists with the costs of water. None of the prescriptions which have usually flowed from these narrow views— bigger and better works and maintenance for the engineers, more predictable and appropriate water deliveries for the agronomists, methods of conflict resolution for the sociologists and water pricing for the economists—tackle the central questions of how, in practice, water is and should be controlled and allocated by bureaucratic irrigation organizations. Again and again, studies suggest that the decisions and actions of engineers, water supervisors, water guards and the like are critical for more productive and more equitable distribution of water; yet until recently almost nothing has been know about them.

The priority here is for research on what may be termed water reform—the organization and management of irrigation bureaucracies to ensure more productive and more equitable distribution of water. Such research is as difficult as it is important. It should include case studies of successful reform, research in the tradition of social anthropology on the lives, actions and rationality of staff members in irrigation bureaucracies, and action research and evaluation in implementing reforms. Such research presents special problems: it may often involve a corrupt bureaucracy, and staff who may be easily identified in any written account. But it is far too important to be neglected and a high priority should be to build rapidly on the work of Bottrall and Wade, especially with action research.

Traditional domestic technology

Little research appears to have been done on traditional domestic technologies for the extraction, transport, storage and use of water. They may have received little attention partly because they tend to concern women more than men. Some possibilities may be: the design of techniques for conserving domestic water for washing, cooking etc., including recycling it through solar stills; the design of cooking pots to conserve water; and cheap storage for roof run-off rainfall (as developed in Kenya); and even, where water is distant, the use of gas balloons to carry water, towed by men or animals.

Water-appropriating technology

The design and choice of pump technology in particular has potential for social engineering through decisions taken, especially about scale, during the R and D process. Larger horsepower pumps favour larger farmers who can then appropriate more of the communal groundwater. Smaller pumps give a better chance to smaller farmers and may generate more livelihoods. Change has been rapid in pump technologies and is likely to continue to be so. Possibilities for the future include solar pumps; pumping systems which use human power more efficiently; improvements to existing animal lift systems; the conjunctive use variously of wind, solar and human or animal power for pumping; and linked livelihood-intensive methods for water application in irrigation.

Water conservation and storage

Among the most obvious possibilities are the old opportunities presented by reducing evaporation from open bodies of water (windbreaks, shade, rafts, vegetation, chemical films), reducing seepage from channels, dams and tanks (the engineer's dream, expensive with concrete and awaiting a very cheap harmless technology); and the artificial recharge of groundwater (still at a rather primitive level). The benefits of such developments might be appropriated by rural elites but they should usually benefit the poor through making available more water for more of the year. It is surprising that there have not been more breakthroughs in this sphere. (It may be noted that such breakthroughs would be no substitute for water reform.)

Slack resources for the poor

Even without land or water reform, water often presents a slack communal resource for part or all of the year. Without loss to local elites, ways might be sought whereby the poorer people could exploit this resource. Some examples might be: in villages with seasonal village tanks, growing and harvesting aquatic plants for fertilizer (either N-fixing blue-green algae, or larger plants); where flooding occurs, anchored bamboo baskets for growing fish fingerlings, or floating gardens; in irrigation canals, floating cages of fish (as proposed by Daget, 1976), perhaps fed on weeds which otherwise would harbour bilharzia host snails; with dams, cultivation on the seasonal draw-down margin; or in villages, the impounding and use (for fish farming, for irrigation) of run-off water from the village area. Particular attention might be given to the seasonality of the slack resource. Often it may be that it is slack and exploitable during and following rains, at precisely the time of year when the poorer people may be shortest of food and therefore likely to benefit most.

The most evident conclusion is the humbling one that we have much to learn. This applies between disciplines, especially between the natural sciences and the social sciences. But more importantly, we have much to learn from rural people who can point our attention in directions which are important to them but which we might not see on our own. Their knowledge and their insights, coupled with open-minded and imaginative research by those from outside, provide the best means of ensuring that gaps are filled, problems solved, and opportunities exploited.

REFERENCES

Barnabas, A. P. *Sociological Aspects of Mahaweli Ganga Project*, FAO and Irrigation Department of Ceylon, Colombo, (1967).

Bottrall, Anthony, Reports of the ODI Network on the Management of Irrigation Systems, Overseas Development Institute, London, (1975 ff.).

Chambers, Robert, *Water Management and Paddy Production in the Dry Zone of Sri Lanka*, Occasional Publication Series No. 8, Agrarian research and Training Institute, Colombo, (1975).

Chaturvedi, M. C. *Second India Studies—Water*, Macmillan, Delhi, Bombay, Calcutta, Madras, (1976).

Daget, J. La production de poissons de consommation dans les ecosystèmes irrigués, in *Arid Lands Irrigation in Developing Countries: Environmental Problems and Effects*, Proceedings of a symposium convened by COWAR, Alexandria 16-21 February 1976, published by the Academy of Scientific Research and Technology, Cairo, for ICSU, UNESCO and UNEP, (1976).

Kuhn, Thomas S. *The Structure of Scientific Revolutions*, University of Chicago Press, Chicago and London, (1962).

UNDP/FAO *Mahaweli Ganga Irrigation and Hydropower Survey, Ceylon, Final Report*, 3 Vols, FAO, Rome, (1969).

Wade, Robert, Administration and the distribution of irrigation benefits, *Econ. Polit. Wkly,* **X** (44 and 45), 1743-1747 (November 1975).

Wade, Robert, Performance of irrigation projects, *Econ. Polit. Wkly,* **XI** (3), 63-66 (January 1976a).

Wade, Robert, How not to redistribute with growth: the case of India's command area development programme, *Pacific Viewpoint*, **17** (2), 96-104 (September 1976b).

Water Supply & Management, Vol. 2, p. 399. Pergamon Press Ltd., 1978. Printed in Great Britain.

ABOUT THE AUTHORS

Dr. Asit K. Biswas is the Director of Biswas & Associates, 3 Valleyview Road, Ottawa, Canada. He advises international organizations like the United Nations, OECD and IIASA, and several national governments on water and other related natural resources development. He was formerly Director of the Environmental Systems Branch of the Government of Canada. He is the author of 15 books and over 130 technical papers. He is currently the Editor of the journal, *Water Supply and Management* and *International Journal of Ecological Modelling*.

Anthony Bottrall is a Research Officer at the Agricultural Administration Unit, Overseas Development Institute, London. Since September 1975 he has been engaged on a comparative study of the organization and management of irrigation projects, with field studies in India, Pakistan, Indonesia and Taiwan. He has previously worked with Hunting Technical Services in Pakistan and Sudan; and on behalf of the Tropical Products Institute, London, in Kenya.

Robert Chambers, at present Research Fellow at the Institute of Development Studies, University of Sussex, has a long experience in research into rural development in East Africa, India and Sri Lanka. He is author of *Managing Rural Development* (1974), *Mwea: an Irrigated Rice Settlement in Central Kenya* (1973), *Setttlement Schemes in Tropical Africa, a study of organizations and development* (1969).

Ian Carruthers is Reader in Agrarian Development, Wye College, University of London. He has extensive planning experience in the Indian sub-continent, the Middle East and East Africa. He has conducted research and published various books and articles on the economics of irrigation and community water supply.

Richard Feachem has his degree in civil engineering and is Lecturer in Tropical Public Health Engineering at the Ross Institute of Tropical Hygiene, London School of Hygiene and Tropical Medicine.

David Henry is an economist and has spent the last 12 years in the international development field. He worked for UNICEF in India for 5 years and 4 years in East Africa. He is now Assistant Director of Health Sciences in the International Development Research Centre, Ottawa, Canada.

L. Douglas James is a California native and received his academic training at Stanford University (Ph.D. in Civil Engineering in 1965). He was associated with water resources planning for the state of California 1958-1964, and in the academic programmes at the University of Kentucky, 1964-1970, and Georgia Tech, 1970-1976. Since 1976, he has been director of the Utah Water Research Laboratory at Utah State University.

Dr. Letitia Obeng is a parasitologist and hydrobiologist and currently holds the position of Senior Programme Officer of the United Nations Environment Programme. She was formerly Director of the Freshwater Institute of Aquatic Biology in Ghana.

Gunnar Schultzberg has his degree in civil engineering and is an adviser with the Environmental Health Division of the World Health Organization, Geneva.

Carl Widstrand is the Director of the Scandinavian Institute of African Studies at Uppsala and Associate Professor of Social Anthropology in the University of Uppsala. He has lived and taught for several years in East Africa and is the author and editor of many books on contemporary African problems.

INDEX TO CONTRIBUTORS

SUBJECT INDEX